P9-DNZ-541

HEAVEN
MY FATHER'S HOUSE

ANNE GRAHAM LOTZ

FOREWORD BY BILLY GRAHAM

W PUBLISHING GROUP

AN IMPRINT OF THOMAS NELSON

Published in Nashville, Tennessee, by W Publishing Group, an imprint of Thomas Nelson.

Published in association with the literary agency of Alive Communications, Inc., 7680 Goddard Street, Suite 200, Colorado Springs, Colorado, 80920.

Thomas Nelson titles may be purchased in bulk for educational, business, fund-raising, or sales promotional use. For information, please e-mail SpecialMarkets@ThomasNelson.com.

Scripture quotations used in this book are from the Holy Bible, New International Version®, NIV®. © 1973, 1978, 1984 by Biblica, Inc.® Used by permission of Zondervan. All rights reserved worldwide.

Some of the material in this book has been adapted from *The Vision of His Glory.*

Library of Congress Control Number: 2014905901

ISBN: 978-0-7852-2742-7 (Revised TP)

Previous ISBNs:
ISBN: 978-0-7180-2130-6 (Revised HC)
ISBN: 978-0-8499-4672-1 (TP)
ISBN: 978-0-8499-0699-2 (TP)
ISBN: 978-0-8499-1748-6 (HC)

Printed in the United States of America
18 19 20 21 22 LSC 6 5 4 3 2 1

To Daddy

OTHER BOOKS BY ANNE GRAHAM LOTZ

The Vision of His Glory

God's Story

Just Give Me Jesus

Why?

Wounded by God's People

The Magnificent Obsession

Fixing My Eyes on Jesus

Expecting to See Jesus

Pursuing MORE of Jesus

Heaven: God's Promise for Me

CONTENTS

PREFACE. vii
Heaven on My Mind

FOREWORD ix
A personal word for you from my father . . .
. . . and from my heavenly Father.

LOOKING FORWARD TO HEAVEN 1
Knowing where you are going
takes the uncertainty out of getting there.

A HOME IN HEAVEN. 11
My Father's House is a home
prepared especially for you.

THE HOME OF YOUR DREAMS 29
My Father's House is the home
you have always wanted.

Contents

A Home That Is Safe 45
*My Father's House will keep you
and your loved ones from all harm and danger.*

A Home You Can Never Lose 57
My Father's House is built to last.

A Home of Lasting Value 67
My Father's House is a good investment.

A Home That's Paid For 81
My Father Himself has paid off the House.

A Home Filled with Family 91
*In My Father's House,
we will live with Him forever.*

A Home You Are Invited to
Claim as Your Own 105
*The invitation to My Father's House
is extended to all, but you must RSVP.*

He's Left the Light On . . . for You . . . 127
*Your Father is waiting
to welcome you home—unconditionally!*

Getting Ready to Move 133
The End Is Really the Beginning

Notes 139

PREFACE

Heaven on My Mind

~~~

~~~

Heaven is on my mind in a way it hasn't been before. The primary reasons are that my mother has moved there since I wrote the first edition of this book, and my father seems to be preparing to move there as well. My husband, whose health is very precarious, may not be too far behind my father.

And so I asked Matt Baugher, of W Publishing Group, if he would consider allowing me to revise this book and offer it once again. He graciously agreed.

As my testimony would reveal, God has always called me into specific areas of ministry through what He is doing in my own heart and life. I can confidently affirm, therefore, that I feel called by God to revise this book . . . for you.

One reason, other than my loved ones, that I believe God has burdened my heart for the message of this book, is I'm convinced our nation is under God's judgment. He is allowing us to be destroyed from within, in every area: economically, socially, politically, racially, militarily, environmentally, morally, and spiritually. Increasingly, it is obvious that there is little hope in our government, in our leadership, in our technology, in our prosperity, in our religions, in our institutions, in our secular universities, or even in the next generation. As I watch all that our forefathers fought and died for being dismantled and discarded, I would be deeply discouraged to the point of depression except for one thing: like a ray of sunlight piercing the boiling blackness of an approaching thunderstorm, the hope of Heaven breaks forth in my heart and radically changes my worldview. Because . . . this life is not all there is. This world is not my final home. Somewhere—out there—Jesus is preparing a place for me!

The hope of Heaven brings peace to this troubled heart, a lift to my dragging footsteps, a smile to my lips, and a sparkle to my eyes. I'm on my way to My Father's House! *Join me . . .*

FOREWORD

A PERSONAL WORD FOR
YOU FROM MY FATHER . . .

❦

I am now an old man. More and more, I cling to the hope of the gospel message that I have preached all over the world. I have preached in times of relative peace and in times of great world crisis, to people in materialistic plenty and to people in great poverty, in countries of political stability and in regions torn by civil war and social strife—many different faces, circumstances, and histories, but all with the same foundational need to know God. Across the changes of a lifetime, I continue to return to the one sure foundation that has undergirded me since I first began: trust in a loving God who never changes, who invites us to draw close to Him in Jesus Christ.

Our age is one of terribly painful remembrances of the brevity and uncertainty of life. When all around us seems vulnerable to destruction and the constant threat of danger, we search for foundations that will hold. We seek answers to the questions that plague us: What happens to our loved ones who have been taken from us? Why are we here? Where are we going?

This little book written by my daughter Anne sets forth the tremendous hope of God's promise that we may spend eternity with Him. Anne's words in these pages inspired and enlightened my wife, Ruth, and have also encouraged me. I know they will you as well. I know of no one who has delved more deeply and prayerfully into God's Word or is more effective in conveying its truth than Anne is. Because of the cross and the resurrection of Christ, we can look forward with confidence to an eternal home in Heaven. The words written here point us to the assurance that we have been given in the Word of God. You can look forward with me, with Anne, and with all of God's children to the joy of My Father's House.

MAY GOD BLESS YOU WITH
THAT HOPE TODAY,

Billy Graham

. . . AND FROM MY HEAVENLY FATHER

❧

This book is developed from the following biblical description of Heaven:

Then I saw a new heaven and a new earth, for the first heaven and the first earth had passed away, and there was no longer any sea. I saw the Holy City, the new Jerusalem, coming down out of heaven from God, prepared as a bride beautifully dressed for her husband. And I heard a loud voice from the throne saying, "Now the dwelling of God is with men, and he will live with them. They will be his people, and God himself will be with them and be their God. He will wipe every tear from their eyes. There will be no more death or mourning or crying or pain, for the old order of things has passed away."

He who was seated on the throne said, "I am making everything new!" Then he said, "Write this down, for these words are trustworthy and true."

He said to me: "It is done. I am the Alpha and the Omega, the Beginning and the End. To him who is thirsty I will give to drink without cost from the spring of the water of life. He who overcomes will inherit all this, and I will be his God and he will be my son. But the cowardly, the unbelieving, the vile, the murderers, the sexually immoral, those who practice magic arts, the idolaters and all liars—their place will be in the fiery lake of burning sulfur. This is the second death."

One of the seven angels who had the seven bowls full of the seven last plagues came and said to me, "Come, I will show you the bride, the wife of the Lamb." And he carried me away in the Spirit to a mountain great and high, and showed me the Holy City, Jerusalem, coming down out of heaven from God. It shone with the glory of God, and its brilliance was like that of a very precious jewel, like a jasper, clear as crystal. It had a great, high wall with twelve gates, and with twelve angels at the gates. On the gates were written the names of the twelve tribes of Israel. There were three gates on the east, three on the north, three on the south and three on the west.

The wall of the city had twelve foundations, and on them were the names of the twelve apostles of the Lamb.

The angel who talked with me had a measuring rod of gold to measure the city, its gates and its walls. The city was laid out like a square, as long as it was wide. He measured the city with the rod and found it to be 12,000 stadia in length, and as wide and high as it is long. He measured its wall and it was 144 cubits thick, by man's measurement, which the angel was using. The wall was made of jasper, and the city of pure gold, as pure as glass. The foundations of the city walls were decorated with every kind of precious stone. The first foundation was jasper, the second sapphire, the third chalcedony, the fourth emerald, the fifth sardonyx, the sixth carnelian, the seventh chrysolite, the eighth beryl, the ninth topaz, the tenth chrysoprase, the eleventh jacinth, and the twelfth amethyst. The twelve gates were twelve pearls, each gate made of a single pearl. The great street of the city was of pure gold, like transparent glass.

I did not see a temple in the city, because the Lord God Almighty and the Lamb are its temple. The city does not need the sun or the moon to shine on it, for the glory of God gives it light, and the Lamb is its lamp. The nations will walk by its light, and the kings of the earth

*will bring their splendor into it. On no day will its gates
ever be shut, for there will be no night there. The glory
and honor of the nations will be brought into it. Nothing
impure will ever enter it, nor will anyone who does what
is shameful or deceitful, but only those whose names are
written in the Lamb's book of life.*

—Revelation 21

Even though I walk through
the valley of the shadow of death,
I will fear no evil,
for you are with me. . . .
And I will dwell in the house of the LORD forever.
—KING DAVID

In my Father's house are many rooms;
if it were not so, I would have told you.
I am going there to prepare a place for you.
And if I go and prepare a place for you,
I will come back and take you to be with me
that you also may be where I am.
—JESUS CHRIST

LOOKING FORWARD
TO HEAVEN

❦

*Knowing where you are going takes the
uncertainty out of getting there.*

"For I know the plans I have for you,"
declares the LORD,
"plans to prosper you and not to harm you,
plans to give you hope and a future."
—JEREMIAH 29:11

ANNE GRAHAM LOTZ

For the past twenty-five years I have traveled all over the world in response to invitations to share God's Word. There have been times, such as my first visit to India, when I have started out by climbing onto the plane with my stomach churning, my knees knocking, and my heart fibrillating—terrified because I was not sure where I was going, or who would meet me when the plane landed. But what a difference there has been in my attitude when I have had the opportunity for a second visit to that same place. I have left home with peace in my heart because I knew where I was going and who would meet me when the plane landed.

In the same way, the prospect of death can fill you and me with terror and dread—unless we know where we are going. Knowing as much as we can about our final destination, and who will meet us at the end of life's journey, takes the fear out of getting there.

As unpleasant as the thought may be, we are all going to die. Death is the great equalizer, isn't it? It doesn't matter if we have lived on this earth as: young or old, rich or poor, famous or unknown, educated or ignorant, powerful or weak, religious or atheistic, athletic or crippled, healthy or sickly, happy or depressed . . . *we all die.*[1]

Still, death can come as an utter surprise. More than twenty-seven hundred men and women went to work at the World Trade Center in New York City on September 11, 2001, and began what they thought was just another routine day at the office. Many of them had likely gotten a cup of coffee, sat down at their desks, rolled up their sleeves, booted up their computers, and begun placing telephone calls. None of them had any indication that within the hour they would step into eternity. For them, death came as a thief in the night.

For others, death can come as a longed-for and welcomed relief. Within a three-week period, while I was in the midst of writing this book the first time, I attended both the funeral of my husband's beloved brother, John Lotz, and the funeral of my father's associate, T. W. Wilson, who was like a second father to me. John died as a result of a fast-growing, malignant brain tumor. "Uncle T" died from massive heart failure at the grand old age of eighty-two. For both John and Uncle T, death came as an angel of mercy.

Regardless of how or when it comes, death does come for each of us. And each of us wonders: *When will it come for my loved one? What will it be like for me?*

HOPE FOR TODAY

Picture an old man, living on a remote island. He is about ninety years of age, and he knows it will soon be his time to die. Like many elderly people today, he is isolated and lonely, cut off from family and friends at the very time of his life when he most needs them. He is frail and weak, facing the great unknown of eternity.

As incredible as it may seem, this man was one of the twelve original disciples of Jesus Christ. In fact, as one of the closest personal friends Jesus had, he was described as the beloved disciple.[2]

There is no doubt in my mind that my father, like John, is one of His beloved disciples. His obedience to God's specific call to preach the gospel to the world has been the subject of multiple books, articles, television specials, and even movies. Wherever I go, whether to the mall, the grocery store, an airport, a restaurant, a conference, invariably someone will come up and tell me how my father's preaching has changed his or her life.

Yet toward the end of my father's life, he has been "exiled" to the log cabin my mother lovingly built in the mountains of western North Carolina. Because he has macular degeneration, he can no longer see beloved faces of family and friends. Because he is so totally deaf, not even the most technologically advanced aid can enable him to hear. Because he is unsteady on his feet, he can no longer walk even the distance from his bedroom to the other end of the house. He, too, is exiled. Cut off. Isolated. Sometimes God allows His beloved disciples to be exiled for a greater purpose than can be readily seen at the time. While I can guess at the reason God has allowed my father to be in this situation, we now know why He allowed John to be in exile at the end of his life.

John had previously been a fisherman from Galilee. He and his brother, James, were the sons of Zebedee who earlier had been called the sons of thunder because they had such fiery tempers. But by the end of the first century, John was one of the most respected of all the disciples. And he paid a high price for his well-known and outspoken relationship with the One he believed to be the Messiah, the Son of God, Jesus of Nazareth.

Exiled to the island of Patmos in the midst of the Aegean Sea, the apostle John knew he would be facing death in the not-too-distant future. This was the very moment in time when God chose to give John a vision of the glory of Jesus Christ! This vision included a tantalizing glimpse into Heaven, where one day God Himself will live forever with His people. This glorious vision has been recorded in the final book of the Bible, Revelation, because John was commanded to write down what he saw. The vision was to be not only for his own personal comfort and encouragement but for all people down through the centuries. People, who, like me, may have been caregiving for a loved one who was dying, or faced daily challenges of extraordinary circumstances, or confronted lions in an arena, or faced the prospect of plunging to certain death—people who would be enabled to do so with courage and *with hope*.

Hope for Tomorrow

Are you facing the future with eyes wide shut, teeth clenched, body tensed, dreading your tomorrows and what they may hold? Do you feel as though you are standing on the brink of a deep, dark abyss of helplessness and despair, caught up in events involving yourself or your loved ones that are beyond your control? Regardless of what those events may be, no matter your mental or emotional or spiritual state, God's vision of the future can fill you with hope *right now* . . .

If you or a loved one are elderly like John, facing death,
    loneliness, and isolation from friends and family,
if you are in emotional or mental or physical pain,
    facing the greatest unknown of your life, hopeless
    for any reason,
if you are spending time in a doctor's office or in a
    hospital waiting room,
if you are trapped in the long good-bye of Alzheimer's,
    or in the living death of divorce,
if you are going to a memorial service or you have just
    been to a funeral,
if you have wept at a gravesite or shed tears in the night,
if you hear gunfire in the dark, or unknown footsteps
    on the walk,
if you are an unemployed worker facing another day,
    or just a weary parent whose spouse is away . . .

. . . then it is *vitally* important to know what comes next. To know something about where you are going and who is going to meet you on the other side.

As I contemplate the deaths of my loved ones including that of my mother, and the impending "move" of my father and my husband . . .

As I contemplate the painful ache in my heart as a result of my mother's absence, and the acute sense of loss and emptiness that will be mine when my father and husband join her . . .

I am more grateful than ever that this life is not all there is.

Praise God! I can look forward with hope because I have the blessed assurance of Heaven, My Father's House.

A Home in Heaven

*My Father's House is a home
prepared especially for you.*

If I go and prepare a place for you,
*   I will come back and take you to be with me*
that you also may be where I am.

—JOHN 14:3

Home for me will always be my father's house—a log cabin nestled in the mountains of western North Carolina with a light in the window, a fire on the hearth, and a welcome embrace at the door. As I make the four-hour drive from my home to my father's house, my sense of expectancy heightens. Three hours into the journey I have the first glimpse of the mountains—a glimpse that never ceases to thrill me as I begin to climb in altitude through the foothills until I'm enfolded in the valleys and peaks of the Blue Ridge Mountains. My journey ends on a winding, one-lane road with hairpin curves and switch-backs that leads me to the door of my father's house.

The old log cabin, the flagstone steps, the nail-studded door, and the well-worn wooden plank floor of the entrance are not what have quickened my pulse or caused me to make the long drive. My motivation is simply the fact that this is home.

Home. What does that word mean to you? For me, "home" is synonymous with love, acceptance, comfort, and security. It is a place where my needs are met. It is a place where I can take my burdens and lay them down. It is a place not only where I can find answers but where my questions no longer seem to matter. When I feel discouraged under the pressure of responsibilities, or overwhelmed by the problems of daily life, or disappointed by shattered dreams, my heart turns toward that mountain cabin and those whom I love who live there. To go home is to be refreshed in my spirit and refocused in my thoughts and renewed in my strength and restored in my heart. How I love home!

The story is told of an old missionary named Samuel Morrison who, after twenty-five years in Africa, was returning home to the United States to die. As it so happened, he traveled on the same ocean liner that brought President Teddy Roosevelt back from a hunting expedition. When the great ship pulled into New York Harbor, the dock where it was to tie up was jammed with what looked like the entire population of New York City. Bands were playing, banners were waving, choirs of children were singing, multicolored balloons were floating in the air, flashbulbs were popping, and newsreel cameras were poised to record the return of the president.

Mr. Roosevelt stepped down the gangplank to thunderous cheers and applause, showered with confetti and ticker tape. If the crowd had not been restrained by ropes and police, he would have been mobbed.

At the same time, Samuel Morrison quietly walked off the boat. No one was there to greet him. He slipped alone through the crowd. Because of the crush of people there to welcome the president, he couldn't even find a cab. Inside his heart, he began to complain, *Lord, the president has been in Africa for three weeks, killing animals, and the whole world turns out to welcome him home. I've given twenty-five years of my life in Africa, serving You, and no one has greeted me or even knows I'm here.*

In the quietness of his heart, a gentle, loving voice whispered, *But My dear child, you are not home yet.*

While I praise God for placing me in an earthly home that at times has reflected my heavenly home, I am aware even now, when I visit that old log cabin, that I am not really home yet because of Jesus' promise to God's children: *In my Father's house are many rooms; if it were not so, I would have told you. I am going there to prepare a place for you. And if I go and prepare a place for you, I will come back and take you to be with me that you also may be where I am.*[1]

Sometimes life turns into a series of struggles, doesn't

it? My life took that turn a few months before revising this book when my husband, Danny, was rushed to our local hospital by ambulance with uncontrollably high temperature and blood sugars. He was diagnosed with pneumonia by aspiration. During my husband's ten-day hospital stay, my father was also rushed by ambulance to the hospital in his city and diagnosed with the very same thing . . . pneumonia by aspiration.

My father was released from his hospital stay in time for his ninety-fifth birthday celebration. The day after my father's birthday dinner, my husband was released to go home also. Two days after my husband returned home, I left him in the care of our family so that I could fulfill my commitment to lead my seminar at The Billy Graham Training Center at The Cove. The day my seminar began, I had a panicked call from my daughter describing my husband in a seemingly life-threatening emergency. I called his doctors and was able to get their help so that Danny did not have to return to the hospital, and I could stay to fulfill my responsibilities. I led the seminar, but the day after it ended, as I was making the four-hour drive home, I received a call from one of my father's staff, asking me to turn around because my father was being rushed back into the hospital with another pneumonia by aspiration. I had to decline, as I knew my husband needed me.

The night I returned home, I had a conference call with my sisters and my father's doctors. I was reassured that everything possible was being done to keep my father comfortable and help him improve physically. Two days later, my husband was rushed once again to the emergency room of our local hospital. The ER doctor sent him back home, but the next day Danny's condition deteriorated to the point he had to be readmitted. Trusting him to the care of two dear friends, I put Danny on an ambulance ninety minutes before I had to leave the house to speak to fifteen hundred people at a banquet for a local ministry. When I walked off the platform, I went straight to the hospital. Danny was diagnosed again with another pneumonia by aspiration. We remained in the hospital and then rehab for the next six weeks. As I write this, Danny is home, and I am committed to being with him as his caregiver around the clock.

As I look back on that relatively short period of time that was crammed full of crises, emergencies, problems, and pressures, my life took so many turns it reminded me of the torturous roads we have in the mountains that have hairpin curves and switchbacks. Those roads can challenge even the most capable driver with nauseating car sickness.

Has your life also taken not only one turn, but a series of switchbacks?

Have you been more sick than well? More defeated than successful? More tired than rested? More alone than not? More empty than satisfied? More hungry than filled? More sad than happy?

When you feel defeated because after a lifetime of struggle, all you have to look forward to is death and a cold grave, look up! The Bible teaches us that God is preparing a heavenly home that *no eye has seen, no ear has heard, no mind has conceived . . . for those who love him.*[2]

Regardless of our circumstances or condition, we can look forward *with hope* as we glimpse Heaven, My Father's House, which is being prepared as an eternal home for God's people. For you and for me.

As a young girl, my vision of Heaven was framed by my mother's assurance that whatever was necessary for my eternal happiness would be there. So in my child's mind, that included ocean waves, mountain peaks, a favorite pet that had died, Sunday night Bible games with the family, sleepovers at my grandparents' house, Chinese food, and a smaller nose! Over the years, my requirements for eternal happiness have changed, but my dreams are still big.

What kind of home do you think is necessary for your eternal happiness?

Do you dream of a cottage by the sea? A chateau by the lake? A cabin in the mountains? A penthouse in the city? A castle on the hill? A tent in the desert? A farm in the country? A palace on an estate?

Over time, my dream home has become much more simple than it was when I was younger. I now dream of a home where I can rest without setting an alarm. A home that's clean without daily upkeep and scrubbing. A home without handicap rails and shower chairs.

Several years ago, the apostle John's words describing the tantalizing vision of Heaven that God gave to him on the island of Patmos came to my mind, sharpening the focus of my "dream home." I was in Agra, India, standing in front of a reflecting pool gazing at the spectacular beauty of the Taj Mahal when I remembered John's initial impression of Heaven: *Then I saw a new heaven and a new earth, for the first heaven and the first earth had passed away, and there was no longer any sea. I saw the Holy City, the new Jerusalem, coming down out of heaven from God, prepared as a bride beautifully dressed for her husband* (Rev. 21:1–2). Just as a bride lovingly prepares every detail of herself for her special bridegroom, God is preparing His heavenly home for you and me. This loving preparation is illustrated by the story of the Taj Mahal.

PREPARED WITH LOVE

The Taj Mahal was prepared as a monument of love. It was built between 1632 and 1653 by Shah Jahan for his wife. Constructed of white marble, it glistens like a jewel on the bank of a wide river. It is framed by four minarets, each one placed at the corner of the red-sandstone platform on which the entire building sits, pointing like long, white fingers to the sky. The exterior of the white-marble structure is inlaid with black onyx in flowing script depicting quotes from the Koran. The interior, including walls and ceiling, is inlaid with semiprecious stones in floral designs that are symbols of the Islamic paradise.

One can only imagine the painstaking craftsmanship involved in completing a project that required over twenty thousand skilled workers and took more than twenty years to complete. How can one imagine the love that conceived such a project in the first place? Even more remarkable is the fact that the Taj Mahal was intentionally designed not as a palace or as a summer residence or even as an elaborate boathouse. The Taj Mahal is a tomb! It was built by the lavishly romantic and wealthy shah for his beloved wife, to whom he'd been married for only fourteen years when she was overtaken by the great equalizer—death. It's sad to think that although his wife was buried in this exquisite edifice, when the shah died, he was not allowed to be buried with her.

If one Indian ruler could prepare something as breathtakingly beautiful as the Taj Mahal as *a tomb* for his wife of just *fourteen years*, what must God be preparing as a *home* where He will *live forever and ever* with His people whom He loves?

Prepared in Detail

John saw My Father's House *prepared as a bride beautifully dressed for her husband* (Rev. 21:2). I doubt that there is anything more detailed than a wedding. I know because both of my daughters got married within five months of each other. My mind almost exploded with all the details. My daughters spent hours selecting just the right dress. Then they had to find the right headpiece to go with the dress—and whether it would be shoulder, fingertip, or chapel length. Next they searched for the right shoes to go with the dress, and after that they picked out just the right jewelry and the right hairdo and the right flowers and the right church and the right music and the right bridesmaids and the right bridesmaids' dresses and the right groomsmen and—most importantly—the right grooms. Then there was the selection of the place for the rehearsal dinners, the menus for the rehearsal dinners, the place for the receptions, the menus for the receptions, the bride and groom's cakes for the receptions, and the decorations for each event. And I haven't even mentioned the hours and hours of poring over the invitation list after deciding on the color, size, print, and style of the invitation itself. Preparing for a wedding can be a full-time job for months preceding the actual day. And all of this was just to prepare my brides for their husbands.

Of all these elaborate plans, no part of the preparation received more attention, thought, planning, and care than the appearance of the bride herself. And despite all the planning and attention to detail, both of my daughters at one point on the day of their weddings became hysterical over their appearance.

I remember the morning of my own wedding day. My mother brought me breakfast in bed, serving it on the new china and with the new silver I had been given as wedding gifts. After breakfast, I stayed in my bedclothes, resting and taking it easy, so I would be fresh for the marriage ceremony and the reception that would follow that evening. Several hours before I was to leave the house to go to the church, I began to get ready. I started with my makeup, carefully applying it in order to enhance any physical beauty I might have and hide the many flaws I did have! I worked on my hair, sweeping it up so it would stay under the veil yet be visible enough to frame my face. Finally my mother came to my room and helped me get into my wedding gown, fastening the dozens of small buttons up the back and adjusting the chapel-length veil. When I had done everything I knew to do to get myself ready, I just stood in front of the full-length mirror and gazed at the young woman enveloped in ivory silk and lace who was reflected in it. I was tense and eager as I wondered, after six and a half months of preparation, if I would be beautiful and desirable to my husband.

As elaborate as my preparations were as a bride seeking to be beautiful for my husband, they were feeble in comparison with the Lord God's preparations for His bride, beginning with the very first earthly home. The first book in the Bible, Genesis, gives us an unforgettable picture of the Lord God. After at least five "days" of intensely creative work, He *planted a garden in the east, in Eden; and there he put the man he had formed. And the LORD God made all kinds of trees grow out of the ground—trees that were pleasing to the eye.*[3] In my mind's eye, I can see Him on His hands and knees, grubbing in the dirt, planting trees and flowers and shrubs and grass, watering and pruning and landscaping. God Himself was the first homemaker, preparing a place for His children, Adam and Eve, that would be pleasing to the eye. We can only imagine the joyful eagerness of the divine Gardener as He presented Adam with his lovingly prepared home that was not just adequate or sufficient to meet his needs but extravagant in its lush beauty and comfort.

But the preparations made for that first earthly home, like the preparations I made for my wedding, or my daughters made for their weddings, or like the shah made for his beloved wife's tomb, are nothing compared with the preparations being made for our heavenly home.

PREPARED FOR YOU

Jesus promised, *I am going there to prepare a place for you.*[4] That was approximately two thousand years ago! In Revelation 21:6 He proclaimed, *It is done. I am the Alpha and the Omega, the Beginning and the End.* What God begins, He always completes. God's purpose that began at creation will one day be finished. His preparations will be completed, and My Father's House will be ready as a heavenly home for His loved ones.

All three of my children went to Baylor University in Waco, Texas, which is approximately a twenty-four-hour drive one way from where we live in North Carolina. Because of the distance, they only came home for Christmas and summer vacations. But when I knew they were coming home, I began to prepare for them. My son, Jonathan, loved barbecued spareribs on the grill, a homemade apple pie, and time to play tennis with his dad. I prepared those things for him, so that when he walked through the door of the house he knew he had been expected and was welcome, because this was his home.

When my daughter Morrow came home, I knew that she loved a homemade chocolate pound cake, fresh flowers in her room, and time to look through home decorating catalogs. I prepared those things for her so that when she walked through the door, she knew she, too, had been expected and was welcome, because this was her home.

Preparations for my daughter Rachel-Ruth were easy, because I knew when she burst through the door with her eyes dancing, she would just be glad to walk through the door. Anything and everything suited her! But I knew she liked lots of my time so she could sit and talk and talk and talk and talk. She also loved any kind of homemade rolls or biscuits or pastries—and especially chocolate fudge sauce on ice cream. And so I had those things waiting for her so that she also knew she had been expected and was welcome, because this was her home.

My daddy also prepared for my homecomings in a similar way. The first few times that I went to the log cabin I will always call home following my mother's move to My Father's House, I dreaded it. Things were not the same. Everything in the house reminded me of her, yet she was not there. Going home almost made my grief more acute. My father must have sensed how I felt, so after a few months, every time I went home, I would find on the kitchen counter a little silver tray with my favorite coffee beans ready for grinding, and my mother's favorite china mug that to this day I love to drink from. In the refrigerator I would discover my favorite yogurt for breakfast. And when I slipped up to the bedroom I had grown up in as a girl, I would find fresh flowers beside my bed with a handwritten note, *Anne, Welcome Home. I love you. Daddy.* While I knew one of his sweet caregivers, Amy Morgan, had encouraged him in this and then followed through on his instructions, I still knew I had been expected by my father. I was welcome. I had come home.

Considering how I prepare for my children when I know they are coming home, and how my father prepared for me when he knew I was coming home, I love to think of the preparations Jesus is making for my homecoming one day. He knows the colors I love, the scenery I enjoy, the things that make me happy, all the personal details that will let me know when I walk into My Father's House, I am expected and welcome, because He has prepared it for me. I'm His child. And in the same way, He is preparing a glorious homecoming for *you*.

THE HOME OF
YOUR DREAMS

❧

*My Father's House is the home
you have always wanted.*

"No eye has seen,
    no ear has heard,
no mind has conceived
        what God has prepared for those who love him,"—
but God has revealed it to us by his Spirit.

                              —1 CORINTHIANS 2:9–10

The home I have lived in and shared with my husband for the past forty-four years has never really been a dream home, but it's comfortable for us. It has had lots of work. It was old when we bought it, so in order to maintain it we have had to replace pipes, electrical wiring, appliances, and roofs, not to mention extensive remodeling from time to time so that it would better accommodate our needs. Over the years, I have turned the garage into a bedroom, the back patio into a sunroom, and the family room into a dining room. After my children married and had homes of their own, I reclaimed what had been their space and turned my daughter's bedroom into a study for my husband, and my son's bedroom into an office for me. For a brief period of time, my home seemed charming and almost picture perfect.

Then my husband's health deteriorated. He has lost the sight in one eye, the hearing in one ear, the feeling in his legs, and the use of his kidneys, among other things, due to the complications of advanced Adult 1 diabetes. So he doesn't see when he spills things. He doesn't hear when he drops and breaks something. He is so weary that he no longer picks anything up or puts anything away. So, while I will always be grateful for this beloved and familiar place, I am not living in my dream home.

But I know that one day I will! I have hope that the home I've always wanted, the home I long for yet don't have, is the home Jesus is preparing for me.

What is the home of your dreams? If you are . . .

    an Eskimo living in an ice hut,
    a Chinese living in a bamboo hut,
    an African living in a mud hut,
    a homeless person living in a newspaper hut,
    a Bedouin living in a tent,
    an Indian living in a teepee,
    a royal living in a palace,
    a tenant living in a project,
    a slum dweller living in a shanty,
    a president living in the White House,
    a celebrity living in a penthouse,
    a peasant living in a farmhouse,

a city dweller living in a row house,
an orphan living in a foster house,
a criminal living in a prison house,
a soldier living in a guardhouse,
a beggar with no house at all . . .

Everyone has a dream—an idea—of the home we long for.

Do you dream of a home you can never go back to, or a home you can never have?

Do you dream of a home with love and laughter and loyalty, with family and fun and freedom?

Do you dream of a home where you are accepted, encouraged, and challenged, forgiven, understood, and comforted?

Do you dream of a home that never was, or a home that never will be?

When did your dream home begin to unravel? When we have been blindsided by divorce or death or disease or depression or a thousand and one other difficulties our dreams can be turned into nightmares?

It really doesn't matter, because one day, the home you've always wanted, the home you have longed for but have not had, will be yours because it is the home Jesus is preparing for you.

As John continued to gaze at the vision of the glory of Jesus Christ that God revealed to him, he must have stood in awed wonder of a *new heaven and a new earth* (Rev. 21:1). What he saw was confirmed by the words of the One who was seated on the throne: *I am making everything new!* (Rev. 21:5). Imagine it: one day, in the dream home of My Father's House, *everything* will be brand-new!

NO SEPARATION

Following the terrorist attack on the World Trade Center in New York City and the Pentagon in Washington, D.C., our nation was gripped by the heartrending sight of thousands of individuals wandering the streets of lower Manhattan carrying pictures of their friends and family members who were missing. A fence lining one of the nearby parks became a memorial wall as hundreds of pictures were posted with detailed descriptions of what the missing loved ones were wearing, of where they worked, of when they were last seen—all in the hopes that those missing persons might be found. As the days dragged into weeks, it became apparent that there would be no more survivors. Just when our nation thought there were no more tears to weep, we wept uncontrollably as a seemingly endless stream of memorial services began and the separation between friends and loved ones was finalized. Each heart-wrenching, tearful good-bye made me long for My Father's House.

John reassured us that there will be no separation in Heaven when he said, *There was no longer any sea* (Rev. 21:1). Now, I love the sea. Every summer, I spend as much time there as I am able. I love to see the vast expanse of sky and water. I love to hear the waves crashing on the shore. I love to walk along the beach and feel the sand beneath my feet and the breeze blowing gently in my face. But the sea separates families and friends and entire continents from each other. In Heaven, there will be *nothing* that separates us from each other or from our heavenly Father. Or from His Son. Ever.

No hard feelings or hurt feelings,
No misunderstandings or critical spirits,
No divorce or death,
No piles of rubble or prisons of debris,
No business trips or military call-ups,
No sickness or weakness,
No dangers or hardships,
No fires or famines or floods,
No wars or refugee camps or ethnic cleansing,
No racial or political or religious prejudice,

No religions or polls or denominations,
No class systems or economic sanctions or human slavery,
Nothing will ever separate us in My Father's House.

We will enjoy perfect health and harmony and unity and unbroken times together. There will not even be the natural separation between night and day because, *The city does not need the sun or the moon to shine on it, for the glory of God gives it light, and the Lamb is its lamp* (Rev. 21:23). Our heavenly home will glow and radiate with light from within—the light of God Himself and the glorious radiance of His presence.

I have been in some of the great cities of the world at night. I have looked out after sunset from Victoria Peak in Hong Kong during the Chinese New Year, and I have seen the lights transform the hills surrounding the harbor into a virtual fairyland. I have seen the lights of Cape Town, South Africa, wrapped around Table Mountain at night forming a vast, jewel-studded skirt. I have seen Paris from Montmartre after dinner, stretched out for miles in an endless sea of light with the lit outline of the Eiffel Tower beckoning like a finger to those who love beauty and romance.

But even in those great cities with their millions of lights, there are still pockets of darkness. In our heavenly home, there will be no darkness at all. No one will ever stumble or be lost or unable to find his or her way. Jesus said, *I am the light of the world,*[1] and He also said *we are the light of the world.*[2] The sole light in Heaven will be the light that comes directly from God through Jesus Christ, and that light will be reflected in the life of each one of His children. The entire city will be saturated with the glory and light of life, truth, righteousness, goodness, love, and peace. Your hope is sure! John said that he was instructed, *Write this down, for these words are trustworthy and true* (Rev. 21:5). You and I can look forward with confident hope—our heavenly home will be perfect.

No Scars

Because Heaven is perfect, there will be nothing to mar its beauty. My husband, Danny, and I bought the house we live in when it was about twenty years old, and we have been living in it now for over forty years. Because it is about sixty years old, there are some stains I will never be able to remove, some cracks in the tile that can never be repaired, some wear and tear that gives the house a slightly frayed, worn-out look. It's just scarred by age. When I visit some of my friends in their brand-new homes, I look longingly at the fresh, unmarked woodwork and painted walls; the fresh, unstained carpet; the fresh, glistening tile and appliances; the fresh, unscratched windowpanes. It's all fresh. New. Unscarred, unsoiled, and unworn by age.

My own body is showing signs of age. My hair is turning white, my face is showing signs of "character," my skin is splotched from too much sun, and my waistline has thickened. There are times when I'm tempted to look with longing at the pictures of younger women in magazines with their wrinkle-free faces, glistening hair, taut midsections, and toned arms. I wistfully remember *when*.

Age has a way of leaving its marks, doesn't it? Not just on a house or on our bodies, but even on our planet. Earth is, at the very least, thousands of years old. Some think it may be millions or billions of years old. And it is showing signs of age. It is getting frayed and worn out. It is being polluted, gouged, stripped, burned, and poisoned, and much of the damage has been willfully and selfishly inflicted by man. But some of the scars are simply due to the wear and tear of age. It was not created to last forever.

In contrast, our heavenly home is going to be

brand-new. Not just restored, but created fresh. John emphasized this again and again when he described *a new heaven and a new earth, and a new Jerusalem,* and once again the clear directive came from the One who was seated on the throne, saying, *"I am making everything new!" Then he said, "Write this down, for these words are trustworthy and true."* God Himself was verifying that all His promises are true.

Scars of sin or stains of guilt can be inflicted on our lives. On our emotions. On our personality. On our relationships. On our memories. Like planet Earth, we can feel abused and gouged and worn out and burned by other people. Does your life show the signs of wear and tear inflicted willfully and selfishly by those who have had authority over you? Have you ever longed to be able to start your life over again? Maybe you can even identify with the following testimony of a woman who spoke with me several years ago.

After I had presented a message to a large convention, this woman came up to me and briefly told me her story. She described being raised in a family where her father and brothers repeatedly abused her sexually. She was so humiliated, angry, and bitter, she grew up to live a very immoral lifestyle. When she finally married and had a family, she abused her own children. One day she heard that God loved her and had sent His Son, Jesus Christ, to die in order to cleanse her of her sin. She responded by asking God to forgive and cleanse her for Jesus' sake, and she said she knew He had answered her prayer. "But," she softly cried, "I just can't seem to forget. What can I do about the memories?"

What could I say? There was nothing I could do except put my arms around her and tell her that one day there will be no more scars. God will wipe all tears away and erase all memories of such sin and abuse. *Everything*—including our hearts, minds, emotions, psyches, and memories, past, present, and future—will be made new.[3]

However, until then God does give us encouragement. His reassurance is illustrated by this true story that took place years ago in the Highlands of Scotland. A group of fishermen sat around a table in a small pub, telling their "fish stories." As one of the men flung out his arms to more vividly describe the fish that got away, he accidentally hit the tray of drinks that the young barmaid was bringing to the table. The tray and the drinks sailed through the air, crash-landing against the newly white-washed wall. As the sound of smashed glass and splashing beer permeated the room, the pub became silent as all eyes turned to the ugly brown stain that was forming on the wall.

Before anyone could recover from the startling interruption, a guest who had been sitting quietly by himself in the corner jumped up, pulled a piece of charcoal from his pocket, and began to quickly sketch around the ugly brown stain. To the amazement of everyone present, right before their eyes the stain was transformed into a magnificent stag with antlers outstretched, racing across a highland meadow. Then the guest signed his impromptu work of art. His name was Sir Edwin Landseer, Great Britain's foremost wildlife artist.

God transforms lives as Sir Landseer transformed the ugly mess on that pub wall. What ugly brown stain does your life bear? Like the woman at the convention, were you abused as a child? Have you abused someone else's child? Or your own? Have you been raped? Have you been the victim of a violent crime? Have you had an abortion? Or performed one? Have you committed adultery? Or seduced someone else to do so? Is there a nasty addiction in your life to drugs? Alcohol? Pornography?

Regardless of what the stain is, submit it to God. You must be willing to turn away from any and all sin. Period.

Then God excels in transforming ugly brown stains into beauty marks when we surrender them to Him. He will bring peace and freedom to you and glory to Himself. And when we get to Heaven there will be no more scars and no more suffering of any kind, including the kind that inflicted the wound that has scarred your life.

No Suffering

Heaven will not only *look* fresh and new, it will *feel* fresh and new. John gives us, not just a vision of Heaven's fresh beauty, but a "feel" of Heaven's serenity, which permeates the atmosphere because God is there: *And I heard a loud voice from the throne saying, "Now the dwelling of God is with men, and he will live with them. They will be his people, and God himself will be with them and be their God. He will wipe every tear from their eyes. There will be no more death or mourning or crying or pain, for the old order of things has passed away"* (Rev. 21:3–4).

In what way are you suffering? It doesn't matter if you are suffering physically, emotionally, mentally, financially, materially, relationally, socially, spiritually—one day, God Himself will take your face in His hands and gently wipe away your tears as He reassures you there will be no more suffering in My Father's House.

There will be no more betrayals or backstabbings, slander or sex-trafficking, lies or liars.

There will be no more hospitals, death, or funerals; walkers, canes, or wheelchairs; ventilators, respirators, or IVs.

There will be no more suicide bombers or fiery infernos, broken homes or broken hearts, broken lives or broken dreams.

There will be no more mental retardation or physical handicaps, muscular dystrophy or multiple sclerosis, blindness or lameness, deafness or sickness.

There will be no more Parkinson's disease or heart disease, food allergies or autoimmune disease, diabetes or arthritis, cataracts or paralysis, MRIs or dialysis.

There will be no more cancer or chemo or radiation; tumors or tremors or terrorizing trauma.

There will be no more guns in schools. No more guns! Or terrorists or missiles or air strikes or predatory drones or car bombs. No more bombs!

There will be no more war!

Make your own list of what *there will not* be in Heaven. Because there will be no more suffering or that which has caused it in your life.

Start looking forward now with hope, because one day there will be no more separation, no more scars, and no more suffering in My Father's House. One day you will live in the home of your dreams.

A Home That Is Safe

*My Father's House will keep you and your
loved ones from all harm and danger.*

It had a great, high wall.

—Revelation 21:12

On September 11, 2001, like millions of other Americans, I sat glued to my television set. The horrifying scenes of the jetliners crashing into the trade towers and the Pentagon, the erupting fireballs, and the imploding buildings that were played over and over again are indelibly frozen in my mind's eye.

And once again, on December 14, 2012, I found my eyes riveted to my television screen. This time the scene that unfolded was almost more horrific than 9/11, if that were possible, because our nation wasn't being attacked by foreign religious fanatics. Our children were being attacked by what appeared to be an insane young man, Adam Lanza. Before he turned his gun on himself, he had managed to shoot his way into the Sandy Hook Elementary School, killing twenty six- and seven-year-old students and six adults.

Such a rampage was surely conceived in Hell and carried out under demonic influence. Whether or not it was contagious remains to be determined, but there do seem to be more and more random acts of violence. From Moscow to Philadelphia, Norway to Georgia, Arizona, Colorado, or New Mexico, killers are acting out their anger and aggression in unthinkable ways.

As a parent or grandparent, how do we face our teary, terrified children who pleadingly ask, "Mommy, Daddy, are we going to die too? Will we be safe?" How do we answer? Do we speak the truth? Or do we just give hollow words of comfort because we have no answers?

While we cannot guarantee the safety of our children, our grandchildren, ourselves, or anyone else in this life, Jesus Christ does guarantee our safety in eternity. When you and I place our faith in Him as our Savior and yield our lives to Him as Lord, God promises that we *shall not perish but have eternal life.*[1] And the "eternal life" will be lived with God and His family in My Father's House!

In Revelation 21 the apostle John describes the glimpse he was given into God's heavenly home. My Father's House is real. It is not:

An abstract idea,
A small child's fantasy,
An artist's concept of celestial beauty,
A musician's theme for a symphony
Or a fearful person's imaginative escape from harm.

It is an actual, physical, literal place in which you and your loved ones will be happy, healthy, and safe—forever.

The angel who took John on a guided tour literally measured the dimensions of Heaven, emphasizing that it is indeed a literal, specific, physical, actual place: *The angel who talked with me had a measuring rod of gold to measure the city, its gates and its walls* (Rev. 21:15). The city he measured was exceedingly large.

Have you ever felt trapped in a small home? A dormitory room? A hospital bed? A wheelchair? An office cubicle? A prison cell?

Three times a week, my husband reclines on a bed for five hours at a time in a dialysis clinic as his blood is removed, cleansed, then replaced. While he hates the feeling of being trapped, his life depends on it because he has advanced renal failure.

I can assure you, my husband is looking forward to

My Father's House. A very real place in which he will enjoy very real freedom from not only dialysis but all the complications of diabetes. He will never again fear an MRSA infection, or a dialysis port that clogs, or painful needles and probing hands. He will be safe. And so will you.

You will never need to fear hijackers or bombers, terrorists or threats, lawsuits or gunshots, bullets or bandits, boundaries that move, razor wire that imprisons, roadblocks that impede, walls that close in, planes that crash, and buildings that implode.

A SPACIOUS HOME

The angel who was giving the apostle John a guided tour of My Father's House measured off a home that was so spacious as to be almost beyond our comprehension. Although it remains to be seen if the measurements John recorded can be taken literally, Dr. Henry Morris, in his book *The Revelation Record*, has calculated them mathematically.[2] They describe a cube that is fifteen hundred miles square, which is as large as the area from Canada to Mexico, and from the Atlantic Ocean to the Rockies.

It could easily accommodate twenty billion residents, each having his or her own private seventy-five-acre cube or room or mansion. This would still leave plenty of room for streets, parks, and public buildings. Heaven is a big place! *In my Father's house are many rooms*—room enough for anyone and everyone who chooses to be a member of God's family.[3] So please feel free to invite your entire family—including in-laws and outlaws, every one of your friends, all of your neighbors, the total population of your city, your state, your nation—everybody in the whole wide world. There is room for everyone who wants to go.

Heaven is a great big place that is real. It is an actual place that can be felt and seen and measured. As we progressively destroy planet Earth, it is exciting to contemplate that somewhere in the universe, at this very moment, our heavenly home is being prepared for us. As this world ends, a new world begins.

From time to time people have asked me, and I have wondered myself, what Heaven will be like. With no sea, will it be less enjoyable than earth and its mighty oceans? With no sunsets or sunrises or full moons or shooting stars, will it be less beautiful than the vast expanse that spreads over our earthly home? I wonder . . . then I remember that Jesus knows exactly what brings me pleasure and joy. The

Creator who created all the earthly beauty we have grown to love . . .

> The majestic snowcapped peaks of the Alps,
> The rushing mountain streams,
> The brilliantly colored fall leaves,
> The carpets of wildflowers,
> The glistening fin of a fish as it leaps out of a
> sparkling sea,
> The graceful gliding of a swan across the lake,
> The lilting notes of a canary's song,
> The whir of a hummingbird's wings,
> The shimmer of the dew on the grass in early
> morning . . .

This is the *same* Creator who has prepared our heavenly home for us. If God could make the heavens and earth as beautiful as we think they are today—which includes thousands of years of wear and tear, corruption and pollution, sin and selfishness—can you imagine what the new Heaven and the new earth will look like? It will be much more glorious than any eyes have seen, any ears have heard, or any minds have ever conceived.[4] John saw it . . .

A Secure Home

John gazed on *a great, high wall . . . made of jasper* that surrounds our future home (Rev. 21:12, 18). The wall is described as being over two hundred feet thick and made of a gemstone resembling a diamond. It's hard to imagine the beauty of two-hundred-foot-thick walls made of "diamonds" that reflect the light of God. Or to imagine the safety of those who live inside walls that are two hundred feet thick. The walls are so strong that God's loved ones will be eternally secure.

Have you ever been the victim of a violent crime? A drive-by shooting? Rape? Robbery? Mugging? Has one of your children ever been the victim of a violent crime or perhaps been involved in a tragic car accident?

Several years ago my husband and I were cruising the Aegean Sea on a beautiful ship as the guests of friends when I received word that the captain on the bridge wished to speak with me. When I went up, he told me I had an incoming phone call on the ship's radio. When I answered and identified myself, a young man's voice came over the receiver. He was the son of a dear friend who had been a tennis buddy and member of my Bible class.

He told me that his mother and father had been walking in the cool of the evening down their little country lane when a car that was passing by suddenly swerved, taking the life of his mother. He was calling to ask me to speak at her funeral. I agreed.

Shortly after arriving home, I stood in front of a packed church overflowing with shocked, grieving friends and family members. As simply as I could, I told them about My Father's House where my friend had gone to live forever. And I took comfort in knowing she was safely inside those two-hundred-foot-thick walls.

When my three children were growing up, I did all I knew to do to ensure their safety. Childproof caps on medicines, chemicals up out of reach, seat belts securely fastened, hands tightly held as we walked, stern warnings about fire and electrical outlets, all were part of the normal, daily routine. When they grew up they went off to college, then to other homes and cities where I could not supervise. There was no way of tracking moment by moment what they were involved in or who they were involved with. But I had a deep peace because all of my children, when they were young, had placed their faith in Jesus Christ as their own Savior. I knew they had been born again into the family of God and therefore,

My Father's House is also their own. Regardless of what happened here in this life, I knew they were, and are, eternally secure.

What have you done to ensure that your children will be safe in eternity? Don't leave the issue of your child's eternal safety up to the church, or a school, or a "professional" religious leader. It's your responsibility and privilege to tell your children about God, about their own sin, about their need to claim Jesus Christ as their Savior so their sins will be washed away, about their Father's House and how to get there. If for any reason you no longer have their "ear," then pray, trusting God for the safety He will one day provide for you and asking Him to bring your children to the point that they will claim My Father's House as their own.

When I read of overcrowded slums, disintegrating shantytowns, sweatshops, or slave labor; of drug addictions, sex trafficking, gang rapes, or pedophiles; of drive-by shootings, terrorist attacks, missile strikes, or military invasions; of earthquakes and the tremors of their aftershocks; of rivers of molten lava incinerating villages; stock market fluctuations that rob the elderly of their retirement, or financial failures that bankrupt businesses, or government corruption that takes advantage of the oppressed; of incurable diseases, untimely deaths,

mysterious disappearances, or violent robberies; of racial
hatred, social injustice, political oppression, or weapons
of mass destruction; of germ warfare, massive relocation,
or refugee camps . . . my heart burns with righteous anger
even as it is broken. My tears flow freely, while I choose to
look up and praise God for My Father's House, which is
safe and secure—forever.

A HOME YOU CAN NEVER LOSE

❧

My Father's House is built to last.

Therefore,
since we are receiving a kingdom that cannot be shaken,
let us be thankful,
and so worship God acceptably with reverence and awe.

—HEBREWS 12:28

My husband has played basketball all of his life. He grew up playing in the streets of New York City, in backyard lots, on playground courts, and even in an old barn his father had converted for that purpose. One of his childhood dreams was realized when he was given a four-year scholarship to play at a major university. The second year he played at the university, his team went undefeated for thirty-two straight games. Not only did they win the NCAA national championship, but their season set an all-time record that still stands. It was the accomplishment of a lifelong goal that had consumed hours and hours of time, effort, and energy. Danny describes the experience of winning that final game for the national championship—in triple overtime—as a thrill he had never experienced before or since. But within a few short hours, the thrill was gone, an emptiness set in, and he wondered, *Is this all there is?* A dust-collecting plaque, a few newspaper clippings that have grown yellow, and memories that have faded with time are all that are left of the thrill that was the dream and achievement of a lifetime.

When the game of life is over and we step into eternity, I wonder how many people will have that same empty feeling of, *Is this all there is? Is this all there is to my life's work and dreams and achievements?* The hard-earned degrees, the fought-for position, the worldwide reputation, the accumulated wealth, the bulging résumé, the designer homes, the fashionable clothes, the collector's art, the priceless jewels, the exotic trips, the gourmet meals, the toned physique . . . all will one day disintegrate into eternal nothingness. Will your life have been wasted because it had no real eternal significance? Will you shake your head as you look back on the ashes of your wasted life and groan, *Is this all there is to show for a lifetime of living and hard work? What was it all for, anyway?*

Fulfillment and satisfaction can be very temporary and fleeting. The emptiness of having lived a wasted life can be illustrated by the discouragement of building a new house or remodeling an old one, only to find, a year after the project is finished, that the roof leaks, the floors creak, the plumbing breaks, the windows stick, and it just generally does not hold up to the wear and tear of day-to-day living.

How many times do we hear some frustrated homeowner comment wistfully, "They just don't build houses like they used to"? He or she knows that many older homes were built to last while modern construction can be less enduring.

The twin towers of the World Trade Center in New York City were built in the 1960s and 1970s, and they were built to last. Skilled architects and rugged construction workers toiled seven years to complete the two buildings. The towers were constructed with steel beams running every thirty-six inches from the basements of the buildings to the tops of the 110 floors. They were built to withstand the impact of one of the largest airplanes of that day. But on September 11, 2001, following the fiery impact of modern jetliners loaded to capacity with jet fuel, both towers imploded in billowing clouds of dust and ashes and twisted metal. The twin towers, built to last for generations, had not even lasted for one.

In 1912, the largest and most luxurious ship ever built at that time, the RMS *Titanic*, set sail from England on its maiden cruise, bound for America. The opulently appointed vessel was 852 feet long and boasted sixteen watertight compartments to keep its passengers safely afloat no matter what hazards befell the ship at sea. The *Titanic* was said to be the safest ship ever built. And since it was thought to be unsinkable, lifeboats seemed like a frivolous waste of space. The great ship carried only half the number needed to accommodate its twenty-two hundred passengers and crew. Perhaps wondering about that shortage as the great ship set sail, one of the passengers purportedly asked a deckhand, "Is the *Titanic* really unsinkable?"

"God Himself couldn't sink the *Titanic*!" replied the cocky seaman.

But then, just before midnight on a clear, moonless night in the North Atlantic, the *Titanic* struck an iceberg and sank less than three hours later, carrying nearly fifteen hundred souls into eternity. The great, "unsinkable" ship, built to last for several lifetimes, had sunk on its first voyage.

HEAVEN IS PERMANENTLY YOURS

My Father's House is a home built to last, not just for a lifetime, but forever. As John continued to gaze on the spectacular vision God gave him, he described Heaven as a city with foundations: *The wall of the city had twelve foundations, and on them were the names of the twelve apostles of the*

Lamb. . . . The foundations of the city walls were decorated with every kind of precious stone (Rev. 21:14, 19). The walls of Heaven are actually built on twelve foundations, each one decorated with a different gem. In addition to the spectacular beauty that is implied, we can be assured that Heaven is eternal and unshakable. It's permanent.

Our world is anything but permanent. We read of artic ice melting, oceans rising, the globe warming, clean water disappearing, forests burning, the Great Lakes freezing, meteors falling, as well as other eye-catching, heart-stopping environmental phenomena. But the moral and cultural shifts that are increasingly dramatic are the most unsettling of all to me.

In the very recent past we have seen seismic shifts in what is accepted and what is not. We have witnessed the demonization of a woman for one word she used thirty years ago, the idolization of a pop star for a pornographic display during an awards show, the legalization of that which the Bible says is an abomination, the recognition of relationships in defiance of God's institution, the willful destruction of innocent human life, political deception that is supported by high poll numbers . . . and the list goes on. Truth that is spun, lies that are programmed, contracts that are broken, trust that is betrayed, all indicate that our nation's moral and cultural foundation is crumbling before our eyes.

Every day the front pages of our newspapers carry stories of things that would have been unimaginable ten years ago, but have become almost commonplace today. And the accounts continue on the newspapers' second pages. And the third pages. Our world is a very unstable place. We can never be certain of the future for ourselves or for the next generation. The fear and apprehension of what's around the corner of our lives can be paralyzing. But when we get to Heaven, we will be certain and sure of absolute, total, infinite stability.

HEAVEN IS PERSONALLY YOURS

Each of Heaven's twelve foundations is also engraved with the name of one of *the twelve apostles of the Lamb* (Rev. 21:14), who were responsible for making Jesus Christ known to the world. I wonder what John thought as he gazed at the heavenly city and saw his own name engraved on one of the foundations. What a thrill it must have been when he realized all of his work for God and his witness for Jesus Christ, for which he had been beaten, imprisoned, and now exiled, had been stored up for him in Heaven as a glorious treasure.[1] His life's work was all worth it because it had eternal value. His hope was found in Heaven. Personally.

And I wonder, *How will Abraham feel when he sees the city for the first time?* About four thousand years ago, Abraham left Ur of the Chaldeans, looking for *the city with foundations, whose architect and builder is God.*[2] As he followed God in a life of faith, he lived in a tent that he constantly moved from place to place. He never settled down. He never was allowed to put down roots or have any kind of permanent residence. He knew he was just an alien and a stranger on earth—just a pilgrim passing through to a great eternal city with foundations.[3]

Can you imagine the thrill that will be Abraham's when he bursts through the gates of My Father's House? Will he shout, "I've found it! I've finally found it! I've found what I was looking for! I've found what I have been hoping for! All the days and nights of wandering and living in tents were worth it! All of God's promises are true!" All of Abraham's goals and hopes and dreams—those things that were the driving motivational forces in his life—had been focused on his eternal home, and he will not be disappointed.

One day, like Abraham, as you enter My Father's

House, will you, too, be shouting, "This is it! I found it! I finally found it! Everything I dreamed of and sought after is here! All the sacrifice I made on earth has been compensated a hundred times over in Heaven. The money I gave away, the time I spent in prayer and Bible reading, the job I gave up in order to raise my children, the three jobs I took on in order to provide for my family, the ridicule I endured because I identified with Jesus in the workplace, the slander I experienced because I spoke the truth instead of being politically correct, the friends I lost . . . it was all worth it! I found all I hoped for and so much more—in My Father's House. Forever!"

A HOME OF
LASTING VALUE

My Father's House is a good investment.

*Store up for yourselves treasures in heaven,
where moth and rust do not destroy,
and where thieves do not break in and steal.*

—Matthew 6:20

As I reflect on the untold hours of studying a passage of Scripture until it "breaks open" and I can make sense of how to relate it to my life and to the lives of others; as I reflect on the nights of agony and tears as I wrestle in prayer for those to whom I am sent; as I reflect on the miles and miles of travel that put huge distances between myself and my family; as I reflect on the almost unbearable pressures of being on a public platform, scrutinized by the sympathetic, the curious, and the critical; as I reflect on the stomach-churning fear of stepping out of my comfort zone in order to take a step of faith in obedience to God's command . . .

As I contemplate all the sacrifices required in order to live a life that is totally focused on Jesus Christ and His eternal kingdom, the joy bubbles out of my heart onto my face in a smile of deep satisfaction. While my entrance into Heaven may not be as abundant as someone else's and my hoard of heavenly treasures may be smaller than yours, I know that at least I will not be empty-handed nor will I have to face the ashes of a wasted life when I get to My Father's House.[1] I will have some things—some *ones*—to take with me! Because when Jesus said to lay up for ourselves treasures in Heaven, He was speaking of those whom we would either directly or indirectly lead to salvation through faith in Him. They are our living treasures.

LIVING TREASURES

Gold is one of our most precious commodities. We hoard gold, we wear gold, we invest in gold, we work hard for more gold—we love gold and all of the things it symbolizes and will help us obtain. We sacrifice our families, our friends, our reputations, our health—all so that we can increase our supply of earthly treasures. We want to buy more things, apparently so we can dust more things, so we can break more things, so we can sell more things, so we can get more things, so we can show off more things, so we can rearrange more things—none of which will last.

The city and streets within My Father's House are spectacular: *The wall was made of jasper, and the city of pure gold. . . . The great street of the city was of pure gold* (Rev. 21:18, 21). Think of it . . . layers and layers of gold, tons and tons of it, miles and miles of it stretching out in all directions beneath our feet. If the apostle John hasn't already conveyed to us that My Father's House is spectacular, his description of the streets surely does. But I wonder if there is a subtle message to us contained in his description—a message that my wise mother, with her characteristic humor, pointed out to me when she dryly exclaimed that you can tell what God thinks of gold because He paves the streets of Heaven with it. Gold is really just heavenly asphalt. In other words, there are many things down here on earth that we give a top priority to, which in eternity will be inconsequential and insignificant.

It's sobering to contemplate how much time, effort, sacrifice, compromise, and attention we give to acquiring and increasing our supply of something that is totally insignificant in eternity. What are *your* priorities? As you live them out, will they have eternal value and significance? Jesus commanded His disciples not to lay up treasures on earth where moth and rust corrupt and where thieves break in and steal, but to lay up treasures in Heaven.[2] I wonder what treasures we will have in Heaven as evidence of our work and witness on earth—if any?

It has been said that no one has ever seen a U-Haul behind a hearse! There is nothing we can take to Heaven with us—*or is there* . . . ?

- When my children were young I struggled morning after morning to get their attention for daily Bible reading and prayer. Week after week I dragged them, often with untied shoes and uncombed hair, to Sunday school and church. Evening after evening I read Bible stories to them and tried to explain the simplest truths of God's Word. Eventually, my children responded by claiming Jesus personally as their own Savior. Praise God! My children will join me in My Father's House. My investment in their lives will result in a glorious "payoff" in Heaven.

- The missionary who spoke was dressed unfashionably. He spoke haltingly and fidgeted nervously in front of the congregation of well-dressed, relatively affluent and spoiled American church members. But the report that he gave began to describe vividly what God was doing in a remote, almost forgotten part of the world. When the collection plate was passed, I gave all the

money I had with me at the time. After a few more
weeks of furlough, the missionary returned to his
field of service. He sends me newsletters of his
activities. A picture in his newsletter showed him
baptizing a small group of new believers in a dirty
river. As I contemplated the eternal life-change
Jesus had made in the lives of those in the picture,
I experienced a thrill. I am going to take the return
on my investment in that missionary's ministry to
My Father's House.

• The historic church was centrally located in one
of the world's major capitals. The sanctuary had
been packed and the overflow rooms crammed to
capacity by people who were eager to hear a word
from the Lord. I had just delivered the evening
message when she stood in front of me. She was
pencil-thin, young, with a somewhat startled
expression on her face. With the help of another
woman, she haltingly told me that she had just
come to the city from Beijing, China. Her curiosity
about Christianity had drawn her into the crowded
church service where she had encountered Jesus
Christ and prayed to receive Him as her Savior. I
asked her if she had any questions. Then I put my

arms around her and praised God. I knew that one day I would join this trembling young girl in My Father's House. In a very real sense, I will take her with me to Heaven.

- My daughter ran into my house, clutching an e-mail she had just received in our ministry office. It was from a man on the West Coast who had watched as I was interviewed on national television, and as a result had purchased my book *Just Give Me Jesus*. The e-mail described his desperate search for meaning—something to fill the emptiness in his life that constantly gnawed at him in spite of his busy schedule and multitude of friends. His search had ended as he read the book and focused on Jesus. He committed his life to Jesus and exclaimed that he would never be the same. The tears in my daughter's eyes were mirrored by my own, and I knew I would take this young man with me to My Father's House.

- The package was delivered to me at a conference center where I was leading a three-day seminar. When I opened it, I found a tattered, stained paperback copy of my book *God's Story*. As I examined it, I saw that it was underlined, dog-eared, and weathered, and had obviously been read over and over again. Inside was a letter from a woman who wrote that she had seen a homeless man begging at the door of a McDonald's restaurant. When she inquired if she could buy him a meal, he had refused but asked her if she would mail a book to the author. Then he handed her *God's Story*. She dutifully mailed it to my father's organization, which then forwarded it to the conference center where it was delivered to me. When I opened the flyleaf, I found scrawled across it bits and pieces of the homeless man's testimony. He was a Vietnam vet. An alcoholic. Hardened. Embittered. One of the millions of men and women who wander the streets of our cities. One day as he sat begging, someone passing by handed him, not money, but this paperback book. He wrote that he had been reading it for days and weeks and months. Through its pages, he had found the love of God. His bitterness had been removed, his hardness had been softened, and he had committed his life to Jesus Christ. The book is now on my shelf as a constant reminder to pray for this homeless man whom one day I will "take" to My Father's House.

When Jesus said to lay up for ourselves treasures in Heaven, He was speaking of those we would lead to faith in Him. Our living treasures. But He was also speaking of our own character that increasingly is conformed by God's Spirit into His own image. This is another subtle message that is conveyed by the streets of My Father's House.

Lasting Treasure

The streets of our heavenly home are not only made of pure gold but, amazingly and almost incomprehensively, they are also described as being as transparent as glass: *The great street of the city was of pure gold, like transparent glass* (Rev. 21:21). Surely gold that is polished until it looks like transparent glass would function as a mirror. Then everything that moves or walks along those streets would be reflected throughout our home.

The Bible tells us that when we get to Heaven all of our sins and flaws will fall away, and we will be like Jesus.[3] With our unique personalities and characteristics, every single one of us is going to perfectly reflect the character of Christ. And as we walk on streets that reflect like mirrors, every step we take and every move we make is going to bring glory to Him.

Do you ever get frustrated with the habits of sin in your life? I do. Even though I have been to the cross and received forgiveness for all my sin, I still sin. I don't want to. I try not to. I hate sin. But I still sin. The reality of sin is the single most discouraging, defeating, depressing fact in my life. But I can look forward with hope. Because one day, when I get to My Father's House, all of my sin . . . my sinful tendencies and thoughts and actions and attitudes and habits and words and feelings . . . *all my sins* are going to fall away like a stinking garment that finally drops off and is discarded. What will be left at that point will be the character of Christ that has developed in me during my life on earth.[4]

> When I obeyed Him in the midst of suffering . . .
> When I trusted Him with unanswered prayer . . .
> When I loved Him without having seen Him . . .
> When I believed in Him even though all
>   evidence was contrary to His Word . . .
> When I focused on Him in the darkness of
> depression and discouragement . . .

When I hoped in Him alone to
    bring me through . . .
His character was being formed in me.[5]

When I chose to be patient instead of frustrated . . .
When I chose to love instead of hate . . .
When I chose to hold my tongue
    instead of lash out in anger . . .
When I chose to gently instruct
    instead of harshly correct . . .
When I chose to be gracious instead of rude . . .
When I chose to be kind instead of mean . . .
When I chose to be unselfish instead of selfish . . .
When I chose to give up my rights
    instead of insisting on them . . .
When I chose to tell the truth instead of lie . . .
His character was being formed in me.[6]

When I chose to submit to the pain . . .
When I chose to accept the pressure . . .
When I chose to bear the burden . . .
When I chose, every day, to deny myself
    and take up the cross of His will for
    my life that includes suffering . . .

When I chose to follow Him and not the crowd . . .
When I chose to live by His Word, not
    by the opinions of others . . .
His character was being formed in me.[7]

And it's His character, revealed in and through me,
that will be reflected throughout My Father's House. As
you and I totally yield our lives to the control of God's
Spirit within us, He uses the responsibilities, relationships,
and ridicule; the opportunities, obstacles, and obligations;
the pressures, pain, and problems; the success, sickness,
and solitude—He uses *all things* to work for our ultimate
good, which is increasing, progressive, glorious conformity
to the image of Jesus Christ.[8]

As you and I lay up for ourselves living, lasting treasures in Heaven, we come to the awesome conclusion that
we ourselves are *His* treasure. When God the Father looked
throughout the universe for something to give His only
Son in reward for what He had accomplished on earth, the
Father handpicked you! You are the Father's priceless gift
of love to the Son.[9] And one day He will display His priceless treasures before the universe—in My Father's House.

A Home That's Paid For

~

My Father Himself has paid off the House.

For God so loved the world
  that he gave his one and only Son,
that whoever believes in him
  shall not perish
but have eternal life.

—JOHN 3:16

Before we were married, Danny bought a small home for us, sight unseen to me. When we returned from our honeymoon, he took me straight to this little four-room house, where we lived for the next five years. In order to purchase the house, he had taken out a mortgage so that our monthly payments were stretched out over thirty years. If we had taken the full thirty years to pay off the mortgage, we would have ended up paying triple the purchase price of the home because the payments included interest to the bank where he had borrowed the money. It was a difficult prospect to face, but we were strapped and we could not manage larger monthly payments. He held down three jobs and I worked part-time just to meet those monthly payments. We dreamed of one day having our house paid for.

After five years, we sold the house for more than we had paid for it, which enabled us to have the money for the down payment on our next home. The new house was more expensive than the previous one, with larger monthly payments. With children soon arriving on the scene, I could not work even part-time outside of the home, so we struggled to get by on Danny's income. Even though his dental practice had begun to flourish, we still lived hand-to-mouth, with the monthly payments once again determining the rest of our cash flow. And we kept dreaming of having our house paid for.

But that dream faded as the reality of life set in. All three of our children were in college at the same time. All three had weddings within the same year. And so Danny and I settled in to a lifetime of making monthly payments on a home that never seemed any closer to being paid for than when we began. Like Danny and me, many people dream of having their houses paid for. But it's just a dream.

My beloved father-in-law was a street-corner preacher in New York City. The small churches he pastored on the weekends were not able to support him and his family sufficiently, so he also worked full-time for the New York Telephone Company. He paid forty-eight hundred dollars for the home on Long Island where my husband went to junior and senior high school. When my father-in-law died approximately thirty-five years after the initial purchase of the home, he owed more than *one hundred thousand dollars* on it! He had mortgaged and remortgaged and remortgaged his home in order to meet the needs of his family as well as to satisfy his insatiable appetite for theological books. Ever-increasing monthly payments were a built-in part of his life. For Danny's father, a home that was paid for was, at best, a very remote dream.

The payment for My Father's House began before time when God decided to bring you and me into existence.[1] In the beginning of human history, God created you and me to live with Him forever. Eden was the garden paradise that He personally handcrafted as a custom-designed home in which we would live with Him. But the human race, represented by Adam and Eve, rebelled against the Creator's plan, and consequently, paradise was lost.

Still, the Creator did not forget or abandon those whom He had created for Himself. At a predetermined time, He sent His own Son to die on the cross in order to take away the sin of all mankind, bring us back into a right relationship with Himself if we would choose to be reconciled, and open once again the gates to His heavenly home. Paradise has been regained.

But who can afford Paradise? Who can be guaranteed an entrance into such a place? Maybe saints. Or missionaries.

Or popes. Or preachers. But ordinary people like you and me? And what about less-than-ordinary people? How can anyone afford to go to Heaven? Billionaires? The sobering truth is that our home in Heaven cannot be bought. Not by any amount of money, or a lifetime of good works, or fanatical religiosity, or perfect church attendance, or carefully carried-out rituals, or trusted traditions. It doesn't matter whether we are extraordinary, ordinary, or less than ordinary. Because Heaven is actually priceless. There is no payment we could make that would ever even come close to being adequate. We can't possibly earn it, deserve it, buy it, or work hard for it.

The glorious good news is that our home in Heaven has already been bought and paid for in full. For me . . . and *for you!* The price has been paid. All of it. You don't owe a thing. Nothing! *Ever!* Why? Because the blood . . . the life . . . the death of the Father's own dear Son is sufficient. We don't pay anything. All we have to do is to receive Heaven as a free gift that is our birthright when we are born again into God's family through faith in Jesus Christ.

So . . . if you are struggling with the monthly payments on your house, or the monthly rent on an apartment, and dreaming of one day living in a place that's paid for but wondering how that could be possible, then you have one more reason to look forward with hope to Heaven.

The payment for our heavenly home is symbolized by perhaps the single most spectacular physical characteristic that John describes—the gates. Incredibly, *the twelve gates were twelve pearls, each gate made of a single pearl* (Rev. 21:21). Can you imagine how large those pearls would have to be in order to be set in walls that are two hundred feet thick? This is especially amazing when you understand how pearls are made.

Pearls are formed when a small grain of sand becomes embedded in an oyster, irritating it. To soften the irritation, the oyster coats the grain of sand with a smooth layer of what is called mother of pearl. As long as the oyster can feel the irritation, it continues to coat the sand with layers of pearl. Which presents the question: What kind of irritation would have been necessary to form the pearls that make up the gates to our heavenly city when they are so large they can fit into a wall that is two hundred feet thick? It must have been more than just a slight discomfort. It must have been horrific agony and suffering.

Which makes me wonder . . . Are the pearls a reminder, every time you and I enter My Father's House, that we do so only because of the intense suffering of God's Son? Do those pearly gates reflect the death . . . the blood . . . the cross of Jesus Christ? Will they be a continual reminder to us of what the payment for our heavenly home cost Him personally? That it cost Him literally everything to throw open the gates of that city and welcome us home. As you and I enter our heavenly home through portals of pearl, will our hearts be filled with joy, our lips be filled with praise, while our eyes are filled with tears as we are enveloped by symbols of His sacrificial love for us? I think so.

So to be candid, I struggle with people who say that the cross is unnecessary. That there are other ways to God and to Heaven besides faith in Jesus alone. That if you just do more good works than bad works . . . if you go to church at least twice a year . . . if you are sincere in whatever religion you choose . . . if you are good . . . if you are moral . . . then God will "owe" you a heavenly home. That there are human ways to make the "house payments." My logical reasoning tells me if there had been any other way to open Heaven's gates for you and me besides the death of God's only beloved Son, God would have found it. He never would have allowed His Son to experience the agony of the cross unless it was the only way to open Heaven for you and me.

And I believe that the very gates through which anyone

enters Heaven will underscore, by their very appearance, that there is no other way to enter except through the death—the cross—of Jesus Christ. Our heavenly home is debt-free, bought and paid for by the very blood of God's only Son. Instead of trying to find another way, just thank God for the gates of pearl. Finally, ultimately, eternally, our dream of living in a home that is paid for will be realized, because Jesus has paid it all!

A Home Filled with Family

*In My Father's House, we will
live with Him forever.*

Now the dwelling of God is with men,
    and he will live with them.
They will be his people,
    and God himself will be with
    them and be their God.

—REVELATION 21:3

On a recent trip to London, I made the time to buy a ticket and tour Buckingham Palace, the home of the queen of England and her family. I passed through one spectacular room after another. I saw hand-painted ceilings; magnificent, museum-quality tapestries; masterpieces of art; priceless porcelains; gilded furniture; crystal chandeliers, and other treasures too numerous and awesome to describe. But nowhere did I see a child's toy, or a family photograph, or an open magazine, or a jacket casually thrown over a chair, or a table set for two, or even a coffee cup sitting on a side table. As I expected, Buckingham Palace is a magnificent showplace, but it's hard to think of it as a home.

While My Father's House is the most beautiful palace ever imagined, it's not a museum or a mere showplace—it is definitely a home. It's the home of the Lord God Almighty and the Lamb. John said, *I did not see a temple in the city, because the Lord God Almighty and the Lamb are its temple* (Rev. 21:22).

THE FATHER WILL BE THERE

The Greek word for "temple" is, in this case, the same word used for the "Most Holy Place," which was the inner sanctuary of the ancient Israelites' tabernacle, and later the temple. It was the place where God was said to dwell. The high priest could only enter once a year to sprinkle the sacrificed animals' blood on the mercy seat in order to make atonement for the sin of God's people.[1] The book of Hebrews teaches us that today *we have confidence to enter the Most Holy Place by the blood of Jesus, by a new and living way opened for us through the curtain, that is, his body.*[2] In other words, through the death and broken body of Jesus Christ on the cross, you and I have been given access to the presence of God when we approach Him by faith in prayer.

In our heavenly home, we will not just have occasional access to the presence of God; we will live in His presence. Every moment. Every day. Every week and month and year. Forever. And ever. And ever.

Before I realized this truth, I was troubled by a nagging worry that when we get to Heaven, you would live over there, and I would live over here, and God would live out there, and maybe one day He would come to visit me in my mansion, then leave and go visit you in yours. In other words, I thought there would be times when I would not be in His actual, visible presence. I had almost a sense of panic in that my whole life has been yielded to the presence of the Holy Spirit, and my entire aim is to be filled with Him in every nook and cranny of my heart, mind, soul, and body. But when I arrive in Heaven, would I have to trade His constant, invisible, indwelling presence for the occasional joy and blessing of the visible presence of Jesus? As I have grown to depend on Him so completely, and to enjoy Him so personally, and to count on Him so faithfully, and to love Him so passionately, the thought of being without Him for even a moment was truly frightening. Heaven became something to dread and avoid and postpone as long as I could.

How foolish my thoughts and fears were. As I meditated on this passage, I came to realize that when John said, *The Lord God Almighty and the Lamb are its temple*, he was describing our entire heavenly home as the Most Holy Place. There will be no place in Heaven where God is not physically, visibly, actually present. Because He is omnipresent, He will live fully and completely with me every moment, as though I were the only resident of Heaven. And He will live every moment fully and completely with you, as though you were the only resident of Heaven. We will each have Him all to ourselves.

In the last few months, because my father's physical condition has become more fragile, a nurse or caregiver is always present. Even at family mealtimes, a nurse sits beside him to supervise his eating in order to do everything possible to prevent aspiration. When I call home, because he has difficulty hearing me, his phone is put on the speaker, so that all in the room can hear anything I say to him or he says to me. I am very thankful for the nurses and nursing assistants who facilitate my conversations with Daddy, because invariably, I need one of them to function almost like an interpreter in order to repeat to him what I say. But I find myself longing for private time when I can have my daddy all to myself. When I can tell him the things on my heart. Ask him for his wise counsel. Tell him how much I love him and how much I miss him and how well I remember such and such. I want to hear him say, "Darling, I love you," without two or three other people overhearing.

In a similar way, I want Jesus all to myself. I want private conversations and private mealtimes and private walks and . . . is that selfish? No. I don't think so. It would be if by just being with me, He would not be with you too. But the beautiful reality is that I will have Him all to myself, and you will have Him all to yourself, and no one will have Him more, and no one will have Him less.

Our Loved Ones Will Be There

Not only will we live with Him, but we will live with our loved ones who have died trusting Jesus Christ as their Savior. I have family and friends waiting for me . . .

My mother,
Lao Niang and Lao E, my maternal grandparents,
Mother Graham and Daddy Graham, my paternal
  grandparents,
Gramma and Grampa, my mother-in-law and father-
  in-law,
Sam and John, my brothers-in-law,
Two unborn babies,
Uncle Clayton, Uncle Melvin, and Uncle T,

Miss A. Wetherell Johnson, my beloved teacher and
  mentor,
Pearl Hamilton, Stephen Olford, and Louis
  Drummond, my mentors and friends,
Kip Jordon, my first publisher,
Janie and Nancy and Ted . . .
. . . and the list keeps growing every day.

Who is on your list? Who do you know who trusted
Jesus alone as their Savior and Lord, someone who has
died and gone before you to My Father's House? While
you and I may grieve, we don't grieve as those who have no
hope.[3] We know that one day we will live with them—the
Lord and the Lamb and *our loved ones*—forever and ever.[4]
That truth brings comfort to our hearts, and is a comfort
that's meant to be shared.[5]

As wonderful as my loved ones were and as much as I
miss them, they were not perfect. And if your loved ones
are like mine, your relationship with them on earth has not
been perfect either. To think of living forever in the same
home with one or two of my extended family members
would give one pause. But when we get to Heaven, the joy of
seeing our loved ones once again is immeasurably increased
when we realize that *all* of us will indeed be perfect.[6] There

will be no more disagreements or cross words, hurt feelings or misunderstandings, neglect or busyness, interruptions or rivalry, jealousy or pride, selfishness or sin of any kind. There will be nothing at all to lessen our full enjoyment of being with our loved ones forever and ever.

On the other hand, do you have a loved one who has died, but you are unsure he or she ever claimed Jesus as Savior and Lord? Is your grief greatly increased so that you are almost inconsolable because you have this deep, cold fear that your loved one is not in Heaven? While I can't imagine the depth of your heartache, could you, like Abraham, trust the Judge of all the earth to do right?[7] Who knows but that your loved one, like the thief on the cross, trusted Jesus at the last moment?[8] With his or her last breath? And his or her last thought?

Survivors on the battlefield, or of an underground mining collapse, or of a shipwreck after days drifting on a raging sea in a raft, have shared later that when they were trapped or stranded and were convinced they were going to die, they began praying, confessing their sins and asking God to forgive them. If the survivors who have shared their stories publicly reacted by crying out to God for mercy, I wonder how many more people who have died throughout preceding generations, whose stories remain buried with them, perhaps trusted in Christ at the last moment and were saved.

Since you understand the agony of uncertainty experienced by those left behind, to prevent your friends and loved ones from having that same uncertainty when you die, make sure they know today that you trust Jesus as your Savior. Tell them that Heaven is your Father's House, and one day you are confident you will live there with Him forever.

THE HOUSEHOLD SERVANTS WILL BE THERE

Not only will the Lord God, the Lamb, and His loved ones live in the heavenly city, but the leaders of the world will also come in and out of it. John described his view of the procession: *The nations will walk by its light, and the kings of the earth will bring their splendor into it. On no day will its gates ever be shut, for there will be no night there. The glory and honor of the nations will be brought into it* (Rev. 21:24–26).

Who are these leaders of the nations of the earth? Since we are told the only ones who enter the heavenly city are those whose names are written in the Lamb's book of life, the leaders and kings who come and go must be redeemed humanity—those who have deliberately, consciously placed their faith in Jesus Christ alone as Savior and Lord. That means me! And it includes you! Because apparently, in some way we don't fully understand, God's children will be given positions of leadership and responsibility in the new earth so that we might uniquely serve Christ for all eternity. The highest positions of authority in the universe will actually be positions as household servants. No matter where our service takes us or what our service is, it will ultimately be for the glory of Christ.

My former brother-in-law's business involved him in a variety of Christian ministries, churches, and para-church organizations. After years of seeing behind the scenes, of being in the boardrooms, of looking at the spreadsheets, of listening to the aspirations of would-be Christian leaders, he had to make a conscious effort not to become cynical. So much of what he heard and saw and read was for the personal promotion and self-advancement of those who masked their agendas in pious platitudes and spiritual clichés, raising money for the "kingdom of God" while they took a 10 percent commission.

But when we get to Heaven, there will be no hidden agendas, no ulterior motives, no secret ambitions, no selfish pride. Everyone—*every single person*—will live and serve for the praise and glory of God's only Son, Jesus Christ. And as you and I enter our heavenly home, we will have the indescribable joy of laying at our Lord's nail-pierced feet any glory and honor we have received.

There will be no painful comparisons and no sibling rivalry and no professional jealousy and no prideful ambition. Every relationship will be reconciled and restored. Think about it. There will be humility and harmony, love and laughter, peace and joy, silence and singing, kindness and thoughtfulness, unity and purity, contentment and consideration. One day our heavenly home will be ready. With loving eagerness and anticipation of our joy, the Father will open the door to His house and gather His children home.

For many years, my husband and I, along with our children, celebrated Thanksgiving at my father's house in western North Carolina. We were joined by my brother Franklin and his wife, three sons, and daughter. As the family grew with our children's spouses, and then their children, we had to extend the dining room table by placing the Ping-Pong table on top of it, and adding another seating arrangement. After a few years, we outgrew the dining room of my father's house. So my father, in his characteristic take-charge, solve-the-problem style, said he would have the Thanksgiving meal catered so that anyone and everyone in the immediate family could come. He also didn't want my sister-in-law, Jane, or me to be so tired from cooking that we couldn't enjoy the fellowship. He then arranged to have it held in his office down in the mountain valley. After a few years, we outgrew his office, and now have our Thanksgiving dinner catered at The Cove.

Thanksgiving has always been a wonderful celebration in our family. The meal is abundant and delicious—turkey with dressing and gravy, ham, green beans, corn pudding, two kinds of sweet potato casseroles (because Franklin's family likes one kind, and my family likes another kind, except now we all enjoy each other's and just eat twice as much), sticky rice, mashed potatoes, two kinds of cranberry relish (for the same reason as for the two sweet potato casseroles), fruit ambrosia, yeast rolls, pumpkin and apple and mincemeat pies with real whipped cream, sweet iced tea . . . my mouth waters just thinking about it! But the highlight of Thanksgiving has never been the food, or the televised football games, or the fun. The highlight has always been the fellowship around the dining room table. As we sip our cup of coffee and gorge on one last piece of pie, my father has presided as each person has then shared what he or she was thankful for. Most of us, including the ruggedly handsome boys who seemed to have crossed the threshold into manhood before our very eyes, have shed tears as we listened year after year to the testimonies of thanksgiving to God for His faithfulness and goodness. As I drink in my father's love and remember my beloved mother's radiance and sense my brother's strength and smile at my sister-in-law's misty-eyed joy and bask in my entire family's gratitude to God, again and again I have exclaimed in my heart, *It just doesn't get any better than this!* But it will!

One day, in My Father's House, the table will be set and supper will be ready.[9] One day you and I and all of the Father's children will be seated around that table. One day our Father will preside as He gathers us to Himself, listening intently and lovingly as we share our love for each other and our love for Him.[10] One day My Father's House will be filled with His family, and it won't get any better than that. *Ever!* And that will be Heaven for me.

A Home You Are Invited to Claim as Your Own

~

*The invitation to My Father's House is
extended to all, but you must RSVP.*

The Spirit and the bride say, "Come!"
And let him who hears say,
"Come!"

—Revelation 22:17

The place I call home in western North Carolina is a big log cabin that sits in the middle of two hundred acres that my mother named Little Piney Cove. Because of multiple threats on my father's life—threats that were delivered in person and through the mail—his ministry board, in consultation with the FBI at the time, made the decision to secure the house and a handful of the acres that the house sits on. So our home now is surrounded by a tall fence, guarded by trained dogs who are also beloved pets, and situated on a mountain accessible only by a narrow, winding road. The road itself is now gated electronically with cameras that monitor all activity in and out of it around the clock. While many thousands of people have expressed interest in seeing it, it is off-limits to the general public. Only members of the family or those who have made prior arrangements are allowed to visit inside the gate.

In the unlikely event that someone would decide to challenge the privacy of my father's house, that person would drive up the winding mountain road only to be stopped by the gate. He or she could bang on the gate, gesture toward the cameras, yell insistently, or cry pitifully, "Billy Graham, let me in. I've watched you on TV. I've read your books. I've attended your crusades. I've even supported your ministry financially. You owe it to me to let me come in." But the problem, of course, is that the person had not made prior arrangements to enter into my father's house, and therefore my father was not expecting him. And so the person would be kept out.

On the other hand, if I drive up that same narrow, winding lane and come to the same closed gate, I would call, "Daddy, this is Anne. I've come home. Let me in." And the gate would swing wide open. Do you know why? Because I'm the father's child.

Just as that log cabin in western North Carolina is my father's home, Heaven is God's home. While it is the home of your dreams, a home that is safe, a home you can never lose, a home of lasting value, a home that's been paid for, a home filled with family, it is only accessible to God's children. It actually is their spiritual birthright. And this is the best part: the Father invites *you*, whoever you are, to belong to Him as His child, and therefore *you* are invited to claim His home as your own.

It's Your Right to Go to Heaven

Inheritances can sometimes be fascinating news. The media will often announce the deaths of the extremely wealthy along with estimates of their estates. Invariably, a follow-up article will appear within a few days, detailing the fights and lawsuits breaking out among potential heirs over their perceived inheritance. One very wealthy woman's estate was pilfered by her butler. A deceased billionaire's carefully hoarded lifetime of treasures was snatched away from his children by his mistress. An eccentric multimillionaire left her entire estate to her dogs! The stories go on and on and cause me to shake my head in disbelief at the waste of the accumulated treasure of a lifetime.

But there is a greater waste that is much more tragic. It's the waste of the inheritance God offers to anyone and everyone who is His child. Because God the Father has a vast "estate" that includes the entire universe and everything in it. He has given everything to His Son.[1] And

God the Son has promised that He will share everything with you and me, as the Father's children.[2]

The apostle Peter confirmed that there is an inheritance being laid up for the Father's children that *can never perish, spoil or fade*—it is *kept in heaven for you*.[3] Although our inheritance may be safely stored in Heaven, it can also be squandered and wasted because the designated recipient doesn't meet the condition for receiving it. And what is the condition? It is referred to in Revelation 21:7, *He who overcomes will inherit all this, and I will be his God and he will be my son.*

The urgent, imperative question then becomes, What do I have to overcome in order to claim Our Father's House as my own? What do I have to overcome in order to receive the inheritance the Father has reserved for me? These are the Father's conditions, and this is the Father's answer:

I have to overcome my pride that refuses to acknowledge I am a sinner who needs a Savior.

I have to overcome my pride that insists if I do more good works than bad works, God will let me inside His heavenly home.

I have to overcome my unbelief that Jesus Christ is God's Son, the sinner's Savior, the captive's Ransom, and the only way to Heaven.

I have to overcome my religiosity that substitutes positive thinking for holiness, rituals for repentance, traditions for truth, and orthodoxy for obedience.

I can tell you very honestly that every time I think through these conditions, if I hadn't already met them when I was a young girl and received Jesus Christ by faith as my personal Savior and Lord, if I didn't already know I was truly born again into God's family, if I had any doubt whatsoever that I am God's child, I would embrace them now. I would not postpone for one second longer getting on my knees in prayer, and telling God I know I'm a sinner. I know I need a Savior. I would tell Him I'm convinced I couldn't do enough good works, nor could I ever do them perfectly enough to earn Heaven. I would reject all forms of religiosity and embrace reconciliation with Him in a personal relationship through the shed blood of Jesus Christ on the cross.

What about you? Since Heaven is off-limits to the general public, are you assured that when you step into eternity, Heaven's gate will be opened wide because you are the Father's child? Are you confident of your "right"? That you will be accepted when you stand at the pearly gates to My Father's House because it's your inheritance? Or will you be like those people Jesus described who would try to just "show up," expecting to be admitted and saying to Him, *"Lord, Lord, did we not prophesy in your name, and in your name drive out demons and perform many miracles?" Then I will tell them plainly, "I never knew you. Away from me, you evildoers!"*[4]

Are you truly, from God's point of view, an overcomer? Or are you an outsider? As much as John may have recoiled from marring his glorious vision with anything unpleasant, he remained true to the directive he had received. He related very honestly that while there will be those who will live inside of Heaven, there will also be those who live outside.

You Can Be Sure You Will Be an Insider

To complete the picture of our inheritance, it's important to point out that there are two places being prepared in the universe at this moment. One is Heaven, which is being prepared for the Lord to live in forever with His loved ones. The other place is Hell, which is being prepared for the devil, his demons, and all those who refuse God's gracious offer to become His child. John was very clear as he

stated that *the cowardly, the unbelieving, the vile, the mur-*
derers, the sexually immoral, those who practice magic arts,
the idolaters and all liars—their place will be in the fiery lake
of burning sulfur. This is the second death (Rev. 21:8). In the
event someone was not paying attention, and because this
is so serious, John repeated the warning, *Outside are the*
dogs, those who practice magic arts, the sexually immoral, the
murderers, the idolaters and everyone who loves and practices
falsehood.[5]

In order to more fully comprehend John's words, consider for a moment the contrast between the two places:

Heaven is a home where there is no more suffering or
death or mourning or crying or pain, as we have already
considered.[6] On the other hand, Hell is a hole where there
is great suffering and weeping and gnashing of teeth.[7] Since
the only time I gnashed my teeth was in childbirth, I'm
going to assume that Hell is a place of agonizing, unbearable physical pain—with nothing to show for it except
more pain and agony.

Heaven, as we have learned, is a home where there is
absolute safety and eternal security within the high, thick
walls.[8] But Hell is described as the Abyss, or a bottomless
pit.[9] Those who fall into it will have the sensation of never
being secure. Of always being in danger.

Heaven is a home that is stable, unshakable, and unmovable with twelve foundations,[10] while Hell is the opposite. It is described as a "lake" that constantly shifts, undulates, and changes.[11]

Heaven is a home in which there is no more night or darkness.[12] In Hell there is a total absence of any light whatsoever. It's a pit where the sun never rises and the light never penetrates.[13] I've heard people say they want to go to Hell so they can be with their friends, but the sad truth is that their friends may be there, but they will never see them because they are in a total blackout.[14]

Heaven is a home where the kings of the nations of the earth bring their glory and where God's children gather to worship Him forever and ever.[15] Hell is eternal solitary confinement whose inhabitants suffer intensely with nothing to distract them from their own misery, greed, selfishness, anger, hate, pride, cruelty, and godlessness.[16]

Heaven is a home where the river of life flows continuously, bringing fruit for the healing of the nations.[17] Hell is a place filled with fire creating unending thirst, torment, and burning dissatisfaction.[18]

Heaven is a home where we will serve God and see His face.[19] Worst of all, those in Hell will be totally devoid of God's presence. Those who exist there will know they were created for God, yet will be separated from Him. Always. Forever.[20]

I'm grieved when I hear someone say wistfully, "I hope I'm going to Heaven. I try to be good enough. I hope I'm living right. But I guess no one can really know for sure . . ." The glorious, emphatic truth is that yes, you can know for absolute certainty that you are going to Heaven! I do. I know I've been saved from Hell. I know I'm going to Heaven. How can I know? Because I've made the choice to go. It's that simple. God doesn't technically send anyone to Hell. A person only goes to Hell by his or her own free choice, which is automatically made when he or she refuses God's escape plan—His gracious invitation to claim Jesus Christ as Savior, and thus be born again into His family as His child.[21]

Some people may think this sounds narrow-minded, exclusive, unfair, and intolerant. But that person is overlooking the fact that God is not arbitrary or whimsical. He extends to anyone and everyone His generous invitation to live with Him forever. However, if you do not accept His invitation because you refuse His only Son as your Savior, then you exclude yourself from Heaven. You squander and waste the eternal inheritance that the Father has laid up for you.

Heaven Has No Gate-Crashers

The mainstream media, as well as the tabloids, had days of front-page coverage about a couple, Michaele and Tareq Salahi, who crashed a state dinner at the White House. As tight as the security was, somehow they were able to get through all the guards and checkpoints to the extent that they shook hands with the president, had their pictures taken with the vice president, and in effect, seemed to enjoy themselves as though they were legitimate guests.

Jesus made it very clear to His disciples that there would be no gate-crashers in His Father's house. None. He described in no uncertain terms that many people who prophesied, who quoted Scripture and perhaps even taught Scripture, and therefore thought they would be admitted to Heaven, were actually evildoers. He went on to add to the sobering, almost shocking list. Those who drove out demons, who got involved in religious service and activities, who performed miracles, who even seemingly received answers to prayer, were evildoers! Using His definition, evildoers are not just rapists, killers, or drug lords. Evildoers may have been religious in their lifetimes, seemingly moral and good. So what determines an evildoer? Jesus made it crystal clear. An evildoer is some one who never established a personal relationship with God through faith in Jesus Christ. And therefore, an evildoer is someone who was never born again into God's family. An evildoer is someone who has all the trappings of religion, but does not have a real relationship with God. Jesus declared, *I will tell them plainly, "I never knew you. Away from me, you evildoers."*[22] He Himself will be the "bouncer" at the gate. He will make sure there are no gate-crashers.

These potential gate-crashers will be kept outside and denied entrance into Heaven along with others listed in Revelation 21:8: the *cowardly*, who cared more about what others thought of them than what God thought; the *unbelieving*, who refused to believe that Jesus Christ is the way, the truth, and the life and that no one enters Heaven except through faith in Him.[23] Standing outside Heaven will also be the *vile, the murderers, the sexually immoral* who called their behavior "an alternate lifestyle" or "safe sex" or "gay marriage" or "an affair"; those who *practiced the magic arts* of the New Age as well as Voodoo, Wicca, and the old witchcraft; the *idolaters* who sold their health, their families, their relationships, their integrity, their character, and their very souls for material greed; and *all liars* (Rev. 21:8).

IT'S YOUR CHOICE

There can be no mistake. Heaven is a home populated by the Lord and His loved ones who have made the deliberate choice to be there. But there will also be those who will be outside. It's your choice.[24]

Are you troubled because you have made some bad choices and the life you used to lead is in that descriptive list of "outsiders"? In his letter to the Corinthian church, the apostle Paul emphatically affirmed the exclusion of certain offenders from My Father's House. With ringing clarity, he challenged, *Do you not know that the wicked will not inherit the kingdom of God? Do not be deceived: Neither the sexually immoral nor idolators nor adulterers nor male prostitutes nor homosexual offenders nor thieves nor the greedy nor drunkards nor slanderers nor swindlers will inherit the kingdom of God.* Before you burst into tears, and throw this book across the room, read carefully what Paul continued to say. He acknowledged the glorious assurance, *And that is what some of you were. But you were washed, you were sanctified, you were justified in the name of the Lord Jesus Christ and by the Spirit of our God.*[25]

Praise God! The invitation to come into My Father's House has been extended to everyone through Jesus Christ at the cross. It's your choice to accept it or reject it. *But when the invitation is refused, the door to Heaven is closed. Nothing impure will ever enter it, nor will anyone who does what is shameful or deceitful, but only those whose names are written in the Lamb's book of life* (Rev. 21:27).

Once again, if you are questioning your own assurance as to whether or not Heaven is your home—if you are not 100 percent certain that your name is written in the Lamb's book of life, then let me share with you a story my mother told me. I pray it will help you possess, once and for all, the blessed assurance of your acceptance by God when you make the choice to be His child.

The story she told me is a true story. In it, a little boy who lived years ago in London, England, heard that the great American evangelist, Dr. D. L. Moody, was coming to London to preach. On the day of the meeting, the little boy walked across the city because he wanted to hear Dr. Moody. When he drew near to the church, he saw that it was situated on a hill. The sun was setting, and the colors of the sunset were reflected in the multifaceted stained-glass windows, making them look as though they were glowing. The sound of hundreds of voices undergirded by a powerful pipe organ drifted toward him. The church looked and sounded like Heaven to him. He forgot how tired he was, and he ran all the way up the long granite staircase that led to the front door.

As he reached the threshold and was ready to open the door to enter, a big hand grasped him firmly by the shoulder and spun him around. "What do you think you're doing, laddie?" demanded a tall, severe-looking deacon.

The little boy told him he had traveled all the way across the city in order to hear Dr. Moody, and he wanted to go inside. The keeper of the door looked the little boy up and down from head to toe, taking in the uncombed hair, the unwashed face, the unshod feet, and the unclean clothes. He then retorted, "Not you, sonny. You're too dirty to go inside. Be gone."

The little boy threw his head back, squared his little dirty shoulders, stuck his nose up in the air and set off with a determined gait to find another way inside the church. But the other doors were locked, and the windows were too high to climb through. Dejected, he went back to the front steps, plopped down, and began to cry.

Just then he was distracted by a carriage that pulled up to the foot of the steps. Out bounded a distinguished-looking gentleman who marched quickly up the steps. He stopped when he came to the little boy, noticing his grimy, tear-streaked face. "What's the matter, son?" he inquired.

The little boy explained that he had walked all the way across London to hear Dr. Moody, only to find out he was too dirty to go inside the church. The gentleman looked at him kindly, then extended his hand. "Here. Put your hand in mine." The boy thought about it for a moment, then he slipped his little hand into the big man's grasp. Hand in hand they walked up the steps of the church. When they came to the door that had previously been shut to the little boy, it was flung wide open. Hand in hand the big man and the little street urchin walked down the center aisle. When they came to the front row, the gentleman deposited the boy on the pew then walked up to the platform, into the pulpit and began to preach. The man was Dr. D. L. Moody!

The only way the little boy got inside that church was because he was holding Dr. Moody's hand. In the same way, the only reason anyone—whether it's you or I or Billy Graham or Pope Francis or Mother Teresa or a murderer on death row or an alcoholic in the gutter— the only reason anyone gets into Heaven is because that person is holding the hand of Jesus. He extends it to you and to me and to the whole world at the cross. And He invites us to come with Him into My Father's House. It's our choice to put our hand of faith in His. When we do,

He walks with us through the steps of life, and when the time comes for us to step into eternity, the gates of Heaven will be flung wide open, and we will be welcomed inside because we are holding the hand of the Father's Son. We will be as welcomed in Heaven as Jesus is! Because we are the Father's child!

I have always loved that story of the little boy and Dr. Moody, because it so clearly defines what you and I have to do to get to Heaven. Nothing! Except to put our hand of faith in His. But the story has never meant as much to me as it did on June 14, 2007, at 5:05 in the afternoon.

My family had gathered at our parents' home in Montreat, North Carolina, responding to the word that Mother had been taken off all life support. For weeks, she had been clinging to life. She seemed torn between wanting to remain here, with Daddy and the rest of the family, and wanting to be with Jesus. We all felt her struggle.

On June 14, as her time to go Home drew near, we gathered around her bed, singing and praying and reading Scripture. Daddy had excused himself for a brief rest. But as Mother's breathing became more labored, he returned to her side. She gazed in his direction, took two breaths, and entered into the presence of Jesus.

My tears, which had been held in check for weeks,

flowed freely. My sorrow and grief were great. I couldn't help but reflect at that very moment that the only person my mother would leave my daddy for . . . *was Jesus.*

I was standing beside Daddy, and I put my hand gently on his shoulder and whispered softly, "Daddy, Mother is in Heaven." And she was.

At that moment, dear reader, it didn't matter that my mother had been born and raised in China, speaking Mandarin and using chopsticks before she spoke English and used a fork. It didn't matter that she had gone to high school in Pyongyang, North Korea—a fact that opened the door for my father to present the gospel in person years later to President Kim Il Sung. It didn't matter that she was Billy Graham's wife. Or the mother of five children, ten grandchildren, and over forty great-grandchildren. It didn't matter that she was an accomplished artist and pianist, or that she was such a witty conversationalist that the United States president, regardless of which one was in the White House, often seated her at his table at State dinners because she could engage anyone and everyone in a lively exchange. It didn't matter that she had written award-winning and best-selling books. The *only thing that mattered* at 5:05 p.m. on June 14, 2007, was that my mother, when she was a young girl, had personally come to the cross and put her hand of faith in the hand of Jesus. I had seen firsthand evidence that He had been faithful to walk with her every step of her life, and I knew, with no doubt whatsoever, that He Himself had been waiting to usher her into My Father's House. The moment she closed her eyes to this life and breathed her last breath, the gates of Heaven were flung open wide, and she entered into My Father's House. The only reason she was ushered inside . . . *the only reason at all* . . . was that she was holding the hand of the Father's Son.

Which begs the question: When have you deliberately placed your hand of faith in the hand of Jesus by claiming His death as the sacrifice for your own sin, asking Him to forgive you, giving Him the controlling authority in your life—for the rest of your life? Could it be that you lack assurance because you have never deliberately, intentionally taken His hand? If for any reason you are not sure whether you have or not, would you pray a simple prayer, something like this:

Dear God,
I want to become a member of Your family. I want to
know for sure that You are my Father and I am Your
child. I want my name recorded in the Lamb's book of

life. So right now, I accept Your invitation to claim You as my Father and Your home as my own by confessing to You that I am a sinner. I'm sorry for my sin and I'm willing to turn from it, but I need Your help. I believe that Jesus died on the cross to take away my sin, and I believe Jesus rose up from the dead to give me eternal life. I open up my heart and invite Jesus to come in and take full control. From this moment forward, I will live my life for Him. I now place my hand in His.

Amen.

The moment you take His hand by faith, claiming His home as your own, you can look forward, even in troubled times . . . with hope![26]

Because your name is now written in the Lamb's book of life, never to be erased!

Because this world is not your home.

Because death does not have the final word.

Because failure is not final.

Because one day your faith will become sight and you will see the gates of pearl flung open for you.

Because, BEST OF ALL, you will see God's face and hear God's voice say, "I've been expecting you. Welcome home, My child. Welcome to your Father's House."

HE'S LEFT THE LIGHT ON . . . FOR YOU

❧

Your Father is waiting to welcome you home—unconditionally!

So he got up and went to his father.
   But while he was still a long way off,
his father saw him
   and was filled with compassion for him;
he ran to his son,
   threw his arms around him and kissed him.

—LUKE 15:20

On one of the first trips I drove back home after my mother had gone to Heaven, night fell as I entered the Blue Ridge Mountains and I began the last leg of my four-hour drive. When I rolled down the car windows, felt the cool mountain air, smelled the damp, pungent earth, and heard the night song of the crickets, my anticipation intensified. As I rounded the last bend in the road, my eyes began to strain as I peered through the darkness. I was looking for one thing—the lantern that dangles from an old birdhouse by the driveway. I knew leaving the light on had been my mother's way of letting me know when I was coming in late, that I was expected. And she would be waiting up for me. But now that Mother was gone, would Daddy have left the light on to welcome me home? He did. When I came around the last curve, there it was, shining like a star pointing me to the front door. I knew I was expected and welcomed home.

And God the Father has left the light on in Heaven for you. When the apostle John saw My Father's House, *it shone with the glory of God. . . . The city does not need the sun or the moon to shine on it, for the glory of God gives it light, and the Lamb is its lamp . . . for there will be no night there* (Rev. 21:11, 23, 25). If you have RSVP'd to the Father's invitation to be His child and therefore, one day, to share His heavenly home, then He is waiting to welcome you. Whenever that day comes.

When my son was in school at Baylor, I knew he would be coming home for Christmas vacation. The day of his arrival was set, and I busily went about preparing with great excitement for his homecoming. A couple of days before he was due in, I heard a knock on the front door as I was preparing dinner. I opened the door to find him standing on the threshold, grinning from ear to ear. It took a moment for me to adjust my eyes and grasp what I was seeing. Jonathan had come home. Two days early. Although he was unexpected at that moment, I threw my arms around him and welcomed him home.

Some people hold the view that if a person arrives at Heaven's gate "early," through committing suicide, even though he or she had previously taken Jesus Christ by faith as Savior and Lord, that person will no longer be welcome in Heaven. I disagree. If one of my children ran from a problem he should have faced, or quit a project he should have finished, or for any reason whatsoever showed up unexpectedly at my door, as Jonathan did for Christmas vacation, I would still welcome him. Because this is his home and he is my child.

There are others who believe if we die when we are failing miserably, or when we are out of fellowship with the Father, or when in some way we are not living a life that is worthy of our Family name, then we will not be welcomed into Heaven. In other words, if we arrive in the "dark," the light of the Father's welcome will not be left on for us. But that is not true.

I once heard my sister acknowledge that she has made several wrong choices in her life. After one particularly devastating decision, she said she drove up to our parents' mountain home. As she neared the winding mountain driveway, she became terrified of facing our father. How would he react? What would he say? Would he even speak to her or be willing to see her at all? When she pulled into the driveway at the side of the house, she saw him standing at the door. As she got out of her car with trembling legs and pounding heart, she rejoiced to see him throw his arms open wide and then to hear him say, "Welcome home!"

Praise God! *PRAISE GOD!* We can do nothing to earn our heavenly home, and therefore we can do nothing to lose it. The gates are open wide to any and all who simply accept His invitation to enter by faith through the cross of His Son, Jesus Christ. The Father is eagerly waiting for His children to come home. And the welcome He extends is unconditional.

He has left the light on—*for you!*

GETTING READY TO MOVE

The End Is Really the Beginning

Now we know that if the earthly tent we live in is destroyed we have a building from God, an eternal house in heaven, not built by human hands.

—2 Corinthians 5:1

I've been thinking a lot about Heaven lately. My father seems to be in transition from his home here to My Father's House. My husband's health is also very fragile, and each time we have an emergency I wonder if he will be moving soon. My mother has already gone on ahead. Perhaps by the time you read this, one or both of them will have joined her there. Death for a believer is not the end of life. Actually, it's just the beginning. It's the transition when our faith becomes sight, and real life begins. It helps me to think of death as a "move" to My Father's House.

The thought of death as a move is captured in the following beautiful and very meaningful parable that I have tucked my daddy's name into . . .

The owner of the tenement which Daddy has occupied for many years has given notice that He will furnish but little or nothing more for repairs. He is advised to be ready to move.

At first this was not a very welcome notice. The surroundings are in many respects very pleasant, and were it not for the evidence of decay, he should consider the house good enough. But even a light wind causes it to tremble and totter, and all the braces are not sufficient to make it secure. So he is getting ready to move.

It is strange how quickly one's interest is transferred to the prospective home. Daddy has been consulting maps of the new country and reading descriptions of its inhabitants. One who has visited it has returned, and from him he learned that it is beautiful beyond description; language breaks down in attempting to tell of what he heard while there. He says that, in order to make an investment there, he has suffered the loss of all things that he owned here, and even rejoices in what others would call making a sacrifice. Another, whose love for Daddy has been proven by the greatest possible test, is now there. He has sent Daddy several clusters of the most delicious fruits. After tasting them, all food here seems insipid.

Two or three times Daddy has been down by the

border of the river that forms the boundary, and has wished himself among the company of those who were singing praises to the King on the other side. Many of his friends have moved there. Before leaving they spoke of his coming later. I have seen the smile upon their faces as they passed out of sight. Often Daddy is asked to make some new investment here, but his answer in every case is, "I am getting ready to move."[1]

No one knows exactly when our "move" will take place, so it's important to be ready whenever that time comes. My prayer is that this book will help prepare you for a truly new beginning . . .

NOTES

LOOKING FORWARD TO HEAVEN

1. See Hebrews 9:27.
2. See John 21:20.

A HOME IN HEAVEN

1. See John 14:2–3.
2. See 1 Corinthians 2:9.
3. See Genesis 2:8–9.
4. See John 14:2.

THE HOME OF YOUR DREAMS

1. See John 8:12.
2. See Matthew 5:14.
3. Over the years, since speaking with this woman, I have been made aware of the effectiveness of the healing of memories. While I am not personally familiar with the

following resources, they have been recommended to me by others as helpful for people needing healing of memories: www.kclehman.com, www.Immanuelapproach.com.

A Home That Is Safe

1. See John 3:16.
2. Dr. Henry Morris, *The Revelation Record* (Carol Stream, IL: Tyndale, 1983), 450–51.
3. See John 14:2–3.
4. See 1 Corinthians 2:9.

A Home You Can Never Lose

1. See Matthew 6:19–20.
2. See Hebrews 11:8–10.
3. See Hebrews 11:13.

A Home of Lasting Value

1. See 2 Peter 1:11 and 1 Corinthians 3:10–15.
2. See Matthew 6:19–20.
3. See 1 John 3:2.
4. See 2 Corinthians 3:18 and Romans 8:29.
5. See 1 Peter 1:6–7.
6. See Ephesians 4:20–24.
7. See Hebrews 5:7–8.
8. See Romans 8:28.
9. See John 17:6, 24.

A Home That's Paid For

1. See Revelation 13:8 and Matthew 25:34.

A Home Filled with Family

1. See Leviticus 16.
2. See Hebrews 10:19–20.
3. See 1 Thessalonians 4:13.
4. Often the question is raised, "Will I recognize my loved ones in Heaven?" The answer is yes. The Bible tells us that when we get to Heaven we will have bodies like the one Jesus had after the resurrection (Philippians 3:21). After His resurrection, Jesus was physically recognizable (Luke 24:31). His disciples were able to examine the scars on His hands and feet where the nails from His crucifixion had been (John 20:20, 24–27). He ate fish (Luke 24:41–43). In other words, His body was a physical body of flesh and bones that had been familiar to His disciples during His three years of public ministry, yet after the resurrection it was also uniquely suited to live in eternity (Luke 24:37–39; Acts 1:9–11).
5. See 1 Thessalonians 4:18.
6. See 1 John 3:2.
7. See Genesis 18:25.
8. See Luke 23:32–43.
9. See Revelation 19:9.
10. See Revelation 19:5.

A Home You Are Invited to Claim as Your Own

1. See 1 Corinthians 15:28 and Ephesians 1:19–22.
2. See Romans 8:15–17.
3. See 1 Peter 1:4.
4. See Matthew 7:22–23.

5. See Revelation 22:15.

6. See Revelation 21:4.

7. See Matthew 13:50.

8. See Revelation 21:12, 17.

9. See Revelation 20:3.

10. See Revelation 21:14.

11. See Revelation 20:10.

12. See Revelation 21:25.

13. See Matthew 25:30.

14. See Matthew 8:12, 22:13, 25:30.

15. See Revelation 21:24.

16. The following verses indicate that there will be people cast into Hell together. However, the physical darkness and torment are so all-consuming and individualized, it will be as though each one is isolated in his or her own agony: Luke 13:28; 16:19–31; Revelation 20:10, 15.

17. See Revelation 22:1–2.

18. See Revelation 20:15.

19. See Revelation 22:4.

20. See Matthew 7:23.

21. See John 3:16–18.

22. See Matthew 7:23.

23. See John 14:6.

24. Please keep in mind that a choice not to deliberately, consciously respond to God's invitation to receive Jesus Christ as your personal Savior is considered by God as a choice to reject Him and therefore puts you outside of Heaven in eternity.

25. See 1 Corinthians 6:9–11.

26. Have you taken God's "hand" in prayer, confessed your sin, claimed Jesus as your Savior, yet *still doubt* that Heaven is your home? If so, I would suggest you pray this prayer for the last time—but this time pray by faith in God's Word.

God's Word says that if you confess your sin, "he is faithful and just and will forgive us our sins and purify us from all unrighteousness" (1 John 1:9). In response, faith says, "Thank You. I have confessed my sin; therefore I believe You have forgiven me."

God's Word says that if you receive Jesus and believe in Him, He gives you "the right to become children of God" (John 1:12). In response, faith says, "Thank You. I am now Your child."

God's Word says that if you place your faith in Jesus Christ, you "shall not perish but have eternal life" (John 3:16). In response, faith says, "Thank You. I have placed my faith in Jesus, and therefore I have eternal life—I now know Heaven is mine."

Take God at His Word. Do not pray this prayer depending on your feelings. Saving faith is an act of your will to choose to take God at His Word. The assurance of your salvation and rebirth into His family will come as you begin, every day, to pray, read your Bible, and live your life in obedience and service to Him.

GETTING READY TO MOVE

1. *Streams in the Desert*, compiled by Mrs. Charles E. Cowman (Grand Rapids: Zondervan, 1977), 305.

Also Available from Anne Graham Lotz

In the *Heaven: God's Promise for Me* five-session children's curriculum, award-winning author Anne Graham Lotz brings her vision of heaven to life for young learners. Perfect for Sunday school programs, VBS, and Christian home-school environments.

9780718021306-A